CONCILIUM

Religion in the Seventies

Concilium 112 (2/1978): Liturgy

LITURGY AND HUMAN PASSAGE

Edited by
David Power
and
Luis Maldonado

A CROSSROAD BOOK
The Seabury Press · New York

1979
The Seabury Press
815 Second Avenue
New York, N.Y. 10017

Library of Congress Catalog Card Number: 78-66050
ISBN: 0-8164-0391-0
ISBN: 0-8164-2608-2 (pbk.)
Printed in the United States of America

CONTENTS

v

Part III
Theological Reflections

Part IV
Bulletin on Confirmation

Editorial

THE PRACTICE of infant baptism (with its resultant questions about confirmation) and frequent requests for marriage in church by non-practising Christians cause serious pastoral problems in many countries. These practices are often not so much signs of faith as the results of a long history, during which the Christian Churches have provided the religious ritual for the key-moments of the life-cycle: namely, birth, maturity, marriage and death.

It has been observed that the growth of the sacramental system was concurrent with a clash and a compromise between two distinct religious systems.[1] The first was the system of the so-called 'four seasons', or the religious culture in possession in many parts of Europe at the advent of Christianity. The second was the Christian tradition itself, inclined to be critical of all ritual, stressing personal faith and conversion rather than any moment of existence, yet anxious to evangelize and assimilate the masses. When Christianity and culture became coterminous, the Church supplied the ritual for the life-cycle by means of various liturgical adaptations. Adherence to Christianity could be presupposed, however weak or strong an individual's personal faith might be.

Christian culture is now a thing of the past, yet the practices of infant baptism, first communion, confirmation, marriage in church and ecclesiastical burial continue. This faces the Church with a dilemma. It can dissociate itself from them, on the plea that its sacraments and liturgy were never intended for this purpose anyway. The linking of the sacraments to the life-cycle has been infelicitous, perverting as it does the meaning of the liturgy. On the other hand, given the historical and cultural facts, can people be left without ritual so that the faith-dimension is taken more into account?

Some theologians, without trying to twist the traditional sacraments to fit this purpose, ask whether in this secular age the Church does not need to develop symbolic rituals to mark the key-moments of the life-cycle.[2] They ask the question on the basis of a deeper appreciation of the secular, and of the anthropological and social, foundation of the Christian symbolic system. These moments have an inherent meaning which is open to Christian revelation. Hence why not find a way to signify this, rather than create the impression of a dichotomy between human life and Christian celebration? This is not incompatible, these theologians claim, with a pastoral effort towards greater faith in Christian celebration. What it could guarantee would be to help a Christian to see the relation of his faith to secular life.

It seems necessary to make a distinction, within the liturgy of the Church, between two types of ritual. While all liturgy is a community act, there are some rites in which there is a special call on an individual to express his personal faith and commitment. This is the hall-mark of the sacraments in the sense in which this term has been determined by scholastic theology. Through the sacraments an individual expresses his sense of God's gift, his faith in Christ and his adherence to the Church. The Church in turn blesses him in Christ's name and sets the seal of the Spirit upon his faith.

There are, however, other rituals which are more specifically related to particular occasions or events in human life. The ecclesial community approaches such events in faith and discerns God's presence in them. Life-cycle rituals properly belong in such a category.

Our present situation springs from the fact that there has been some confusion between this latter form of ritual and the sacraments which mark the moments of personal conversion or growth in faith. Thus baptism gets attached to birth, confirmation to adolescence, anointing to the death agony, and marriage to the marriage contract, whereas these sacraments are not by their nature attached to such moments.

Life-cycle rites, when they do develop, are more prone to abuse, misunderstanding and superstition than the sacraments (when their reality as sacraments of faith is respected). The Church has to keep a critical eye on them. We should remember that one of the functions of a liturgical theologian is the critique of ritual development.

In this *Concilium* we probe the implications, pastoral and theological, of the phenomenon which so constantly links sacraments or other rituals to the key-moments of the life-cycle. The anthropological and psychological foundations of the question are examined. We study scriptural and liturgical tradition for insights into the essential meaning of Christian liturgy. Two examples are taken to show how birth and death are represented in rites other than the sacraments. We look at the relation between Christian and civil ritual, and the ongoing argument about confirmation is surveyed in the bulletin.

David Power

Notes

1. Cf. 'Problèmes Sacramentaires. Dialogue Interdisciplinaire', in *La Maison-Dieu* 119 (1973–74), pp. 51–73

2. E.g. Langdon Gilkey, *Catholicism Confronts Modernity* (New York, 1975), pp. 198–9; Raimundo Panikkar, *Worship and Secular Man* (London, 1973), p. 59.

PART I

Reflection on the
Contribution of the Human Sciences
to an Understanding of the Question

Kevin Seasoltz

Anthropology and Liturgical Theology: Searching for a Compatible Methodology

THEOLOGICAL ANTHROPOLOGY

OVER the past fifteen years serious efforts have been made to relate Christian theology to the physical and social sciences. The task has been assumed as a response to the challenge of secularization. Until the Second Vatican Council, the orthodox model of theology prevailed among Roman Catholics. It took modernity seriously only when it did not threaten traditional Christian beliefs and practices. This theological model stood in marked contrast to the liberal theology of the Modernists which was committed to the basic claims and ethical values of free inquiry, independent judgment, and open investigation of all truth. Liberal theologians sought to reinterpret the basic claims of Christianity in such a way that they might be reconciled with secularism.

A neo-orthodox model of theology developed out of sympathy for the liberal understanding of theology's concern for the human situation, but it criticized the latter because of its inability to account for the mystery of iniquity operative in human existence. It claimed that only theology rooted in the death and resurrection of Jesus Christ was adequate to such a task.

In the years following the Council, the death-of-God movement gave rise to radical theology which maintained that men and women who have come of age do not need the God of Christianity. To the extent that people are really committed to the struggle for liberation from evil in its many forms they have neither the need nor time for a transcen-

3

dent God. The death-of-God movement and the radical model of theology it produced were both short-lived, for in spite of involvement in the struggle for liberation on various fronts, people continued to experience a need for a transcendent God. Hence the nineteen-seventies brought a renewed interest in religion and religious experience.

In order to take account of the useful insights of the liberal, neo-orthodox and radical theologians, while affirming the reality of God and his revelation in the person of Jesus Christ, theologians have recently developed a revisionist model of theology which is rooted in both human experience and Christian texts.[1] Revisionist theology would seem to provide a method whereby the major themes of Scripture and the other confessional expressions of Christian faith found in doctrinal formulas, theological discourse, liturgy, and pastoral practice may be correlated with one another and with common human experience. It would seem to offer an interdisciplinary method enabling theology to relate to the physical and social sciences, to take into account their findings, and to criticize their assertions.

It should be noted that one of the most important areas of theological investigation today is what has come to be called theological anthropology. It is the study of human beings insofar as they are related to God. It seeks to explain the human person in the light of revelation, particularly the revelation of God in the humanity of Jesus Christ. It inquires how people can relate to God's word and his work in the world; hence it also inquires into the nature of the world itself.

The approach of many contemporary theologians to anthropological questions stands in marked contrast to the approach generally taken since the seventeenth century, when theology became quite dependent on philosophical idealism. Instead of asserting clear distinctions between nature and grace and between the natural and supernatural orders, many theologians now follow a much more existential method. They begin with the concrete unity of human persons as they exist in history, situated in the one, actual, supernatural existential order. In following this method, these theologians must be in dialogue with the social sciences and history, as well as philosophical existentialism and phenomenology. Men and women are historical beings; hence their understanding of reality is not achieved in isolation from the cultural phenomena that shape their perspective in various ways.

Although men and women are beings of finite resources, they are oriented toward the infinite. Religion and revelation, then, are intrinsic to the human spirit. The fulfilment of the human aspiration is manifested in the incarnation of God's Word, the perfect union of God and man. The incarnation is therefore the paradigm for all human persons.

In addition to this fundamental incarnational principle, there are several other basic components of theological anthropology. If the human person is ordered in and through his finiteness toward God as the end and goal of all human activity, then God will be revealed in and through the historical and social processes of human life and not simply in personal religious experiences. This is what the *Constitution on the Church in the Modern World* called the process of socialization.[2] It is not merely a secular development but one that has profound spiritual consequences. Any dichotomy between matter and spirit or between body and soul is rejected as a contradiction of the fundamental unity in creation. Although the human person is ordered towards union with the divine, the human person is free to reject God. The unique existential order in which God draws all people to himself does not preclude the possibility of unbelief or the rejection of God's self-communication. Only insofar as the human person freely responds to the gift of God's self-communication does he become fully human.

CONSEQUENCES FOR LITURGICAL QUESTIONS

The positions one takes in the area of theological anthropology also condition the positions one takes in sacramental theology and practice. If God is not conceived as an absolute Being standing over against his people but rather as the absolute metaphysical ground of all beings, then sacraments as sacred symbols are not merely signs pointing to a reality which is wholly other than the signs themselves. They are signs which are sensible expressions of God present and operative within the sacramental actions themselves. The sacraments truly make the transcendent God available to his people; they enable people to share in God's life revealed in and through the symbols. This approach to sacramental theology maintains both the immanence and the transcendence of God.

The foregoing shows that sacramental or liturgical theology requires an adequate method of investigation whereby it can relate in particular to the social sciences, which are preoccupied with human life and relationships. Before the Second Vatican Council, research and writing on liturgy were generally concerned with the origin and development of rites and the theology reflected in those rites. Since the Council, however, considerable attention has been given to the understanding of liturgy in the light of sociology, psychology, and anthropology.

Although the *Constitution on the Sacred Liturgy* referred to the need for such adaptation in a number of places,[3] the *Constitution on the Church in the Modern World* stressed the positive relationship which must exist between the Church and the world.[4] If the liturgy is the expression of the Church's own life in the world, the cultural and social life of the world must be reflected in that liturgy. Likewise, the world must to some extent shape the life of the Church and its liturgy.

The Church does not exist in isolation from the world; it is intimately involved in the whole process of human history. Hence it is not only bound to change and develop, but it is subject to influence from the cultural and social phenomena outside itself. The interaction between the Church and the world does not take place only on the external plane, as though the life of the Church were wholly distinct from secular history. Although the Church possesses an identity in itself, it is dependent on cultural and social phenomena and also on historical events outside itself as it seeks to give expression to its own identity. Every aspect of the Church's life should give evidence of this interdependence, but the liturgy above all, as most profoundly reflective and constitutive of the Church in history, must take account of cultural and social developments.

'Cultural adaptation' does not adequately express what is involved here; the impression is given that the relationship between the Church and the world is accidental and only on the external plane. The relationship also exists on the internal plane. Perhaps the term 'indigenization' is more adequate. It implies that due account is taken of all that is natural, native, and intrinsic in a culture. The theme of indigenization was prominent at the Synod of Bishops in 1974, where the bishops from third-world countries forcefully described the need to implement the process in most areas of the Church's life, but especially in the liturgy.[5]

In other countries, concerns for social and personal justice in the areas of politics, education and sexuality have indirectly raised liturgical questions for the Church. Among these issues are the use of sexist language, discrimination against women and minorities in the structure and execution of rituals, and the imposition of a western, perhaps distinctly Roman, symbolic system on other cultural groups in the Church. In some countries the process of indigenization has been implemented to some extent by the introduction into the liturgy of native prayer forms, readings, gestures, vesture, architecture, and artifacts. However, the process has been sporadic and quite inadequate. At the Plenary Session of the Congregation for Sacraments and Divine Worship in November, 1976, indigenization was discussed at length and the need for in-depth study of the issue by international experts was sanctioned.[6] It seems likely that this will be a major problem for the Church in the foreseeable future.

Modern Anthropology

It should be clear from the start, however, that the problem of relating theology to contemporary culture is not simply a problem for theologians. Difficulties also exist on the part of the social scientists, and among anthropologists in particular. Just as theologians have pursued various methodologies and adopted different models in the past century, so anthropologists have espoused the teaching of one or other school of thought. Likewise, just as theologians have been at times oblivious of and even hostile to the insights of anthropologists, so anthropologists have often been oblivious of and even hostile to the insights of theologians. The need for respect and collaboration exists on both sides. However, theologians should not uncritically accept commentaries by anthropologists on the contemporary religious scene. They may be naive in presuming that an anthropologist's assertions are universally accepted by his associates. Just as theological pluralism is widespread in the Church today, so anthropological pluralism prevails among specialists in that discipline.

Most anthropologists in the last century and many in this century sought to discredit the claims of revealed religions. Influenced by evolutionary theory, they regarded religion as useless and apt to be supplanted by scientific progress. When confronted by the universal phenomena of religious experience and organized religious bodies, they used psychological and sociological theories to explain religion as an illusion. In recent times, these opinions have been shown to be erroneous or at least of doubtful value. However, it is not surprising that theologians and scholars in the field of religion have generally refused to take the work of anthropologists seriously because of their reductionist tendencies. Although the *Constitution on the Church in the Modern World* incorporated many anthropological insights in its chapter on the 'Proper Development of Culture',[7] it was very selective and carefully related these insights to the basic teachings of Christianity. Hence the chapter provides an excellent example of neo-orthodox theology.

In 1959, the distinguished anthropologist E. E. Evans-Pritchard gave a lecture in which he reviewed the relationship between religion and anthropology and complained that anthropologists have been biased in their evaluation of religious beliefs and practices.[8] He pointed out that most of the influential anthropologists in our century have adhered to no religious beliefs and maintained that all religion was fallacious. It is not at all surprising, then, that until recently theologians and scholars specializing in the history and phenomenology of religion have ignored anthropological studies.

Since the publication of Evans-Pritchard's reflections, there has been a significant change in that anthropological textbooks and journals have considered in detail the place and value of religion in various societies.[9] Special attention has been given to religious rituals and symbols. The scope of the studies is broad.

As a science, anthropology is generally separated into two main branches: physical anthropology which is concerned with certain aspects of human biology, especially the study of human evolution; and cultural anthropology which is concerned with social behavior, beliefs, and languages, as well as the shared ways in which people act, think, and make things. Although physical anthropology may affect other areas of theological investigation, it has little or no effect on sacramental or liturgical theology. The insights of the cultural anthropologists, however, are often quite useful to the liturgist or sacramental theologian.

Of its nature, cultural anthropology is closely related to other disciplines, especially history, sociology, psychology, and economics. For some time its findings and insights have been particularly useful to missiologists. Cultural anthropology not only prepares the way for a sympathetic understanding of the people missionaries encounter in their work, but enables them to understand their own cultural backgrounds and the necessity of taking other cultures into account when preaching, teaching, and celebrating the liturgy. They are more apt, then, to be true to the Church's mandate to preach Christ in such a manner as to retain and promote the good that is found in all cultures throughout the world. The implications that cultural anthropology has for areas other than missiology cannot be clearly delineated at the present time. This is due primarily to the ambiguity inherent in much of the anthropological literature itself.

Definitions of Religion

The ambiguity begins with the very meaning of the term 'religion'. Religion is defined in a great variety of ways in anthropological literature, although it is commonly held that religious beliefs and behavior are based on the acceptance of a supernatural world which is thought to exist separate from the rest of the visible, empirical world.[10] Religion is then seen as an objective system of symbols which exists apart from the human person. The theological anthropology implicit in such a view would be basically essentialist and would assert a clear distinction between the natural and supernatural orders.

However, some anthropologists consider religion as a system of symbols which is neither simply objective nor subjective but which links subject and object in such a way that religious experience is personal and existential.[11] They distinguish the natural from the supernatural and do not equate the one with the other. Although the supernatural extends infinitely beyond the natural, human beings experience it in and through the natural. This would seem to be Philip Bock's understanding of religion. In his *Introduction to Cultural Anthropol-*

ogy, he does not deal extensively with specific religious beliefs and practices, but he maintains that: '. . . in most societies, religion is not a separate category or action. There is rather a *religious dimension* to every part of life, and the Western contrast between "natural" and "supernatural" is simply not relevant to the understanding of such societies'.[12]

Bock's assertion that religion is not separate as a category of experience or action would seem to be factually incorrect since many societies do believe that religion is distinct from the rest of life. Whether their belief is correct is another question. The deep fear of those Christians who maintain that the Church has lost the sense of the sacred in recent years and that liturgy has been de-sacralized would seem to be based on an essentialist cosmology in which the natural order and the supernatural are distinct.[13] It is with the theological underpinnings that we are concerned here, not with the experience or non-experience of the sacred. The majority of those who write about the de-sacralization of the liturgy would seem to be forced to reject Bock's definition of religion. However, those who want to draw out the full implications of the incarnation of God in Jesus Christ, his lordship over all creation, and the self-communication of God to all his creatures would tend to agree with Bock's statement that there is a religious dimension to every part of life.

From this brief discussion of the nature of religion, it is obvious that the question whether religion is something uniquely different from the rest of human life or just one dimension of life or life itself experienced at a certain depth level is answered in vastly different ways by contemporary anthropologists and theologians. Just as theological assumptions underlie the assertions of anthropologists, so anthropological assumptions underlie the assertions of theologians. The assumptions, however, are usually not articulated. Hence, the level on which anthropologists and theologians should enter into dialogue with one another is generally not reached.

Features of Religion

Although anthropologists have generally refrained from giving a precise definition of religion, they have discussed its constitutive elements under the headings of myth, ritual, and symbol.

For decades, anthropological discussion has centered upon the relation of myth to ritual, but today it is generally agreed that historical questions about the precedence of ritual over myth or myth over ritual are not open to testing; they are unanswerable. That myth and ritual are inter-dependent is widely recognized. This basic relationship is accepted and in fact stressed by liturgists and sacramental theologians; however, they are apt to treat the question in terms of the interdependence of word and sacrament rather than myth and ritual. After four centuries of sacramental imbalance during which Protestants stressed the word to the neglect of the sacraments and Roman Catholics stressed the sacraments to the neglect of the word, the general stress on the complementarity of word and sacrament and of myth and ritual among Christian churches has enriched liturgical life.

In a very general way anthropologists define myth as a story about the holy. Although earlier interpretations raised the question of the historicity of the story, contemporary interest in the topic centres on the functions, structure and meaning of myths. There is general agreement that myth is the language of religion. It is the sacred story of a primordial event which expresses and constitutes reality and hence determines the existential situation in which people find themselves. Above all myths deal with the peak moments or liminal situations in human life, such as birth, initiation, and death. These moments are experienced as especially meaningful because of their reference to the divine. In other words, mythical interpretations of experience enable people to transcend the limitations of time and place. Freed from such restrictions, they are able to extend their horizons beyond the here and now.

A number of anthropologists have centred their attention on the symbolic quality of myths and the structure of mythical interpretations of reality. Conscious of the extensive literature on symbol, they assert that myths are symbolic in that they are channels through which a society expresses its basic beliefs about life in its broadest dimensions. Their investigations go beyond a surface analysis of myths and attempt to uncover implicit values and attitudes toward life itself. Hence these anthropologists also attend to philosophical and theological assumptions about the world and life in the world.

Modern biblical studies have tried to take account of the extensive literature on the nature and rôle of myth. They have established a basic congruity between the Bible and myth properly understood, since the Bible, as a literary work, has a tradition which includes myth as a literary genre. Since myth expresses in a narrative way what philosophy and theology express dialectically, it readily adapts itself to the expression of divine reality operative in the cosmos. Because myth narrates what exists outside of time and space, it naturally expresses what is eternal and omnipresent. But revelation in the Jewish and Christian traditions asserts that there are decisive events which are inaugurated by God whose existence is everywhere and always but who acts in time and space. Historical events, then, mark God's intervention in the cosmos. For Christians, salvation is historical not only in the sense that it was accomplished in and through the life, death, and resurrection of Jesus Christ, but in the sense that the resurrection experience of Jesus must be communicated to people who live here and now. In the liturgical year, the life, death and resurrection of Jesus are celebrated not in the sense that the narration of the events repeats the historical events themselves but in the sense that the effect achieved in the historical events is made present and operative in the life of people living after the time of Christ. Myth and fact are both demanded by the revelation of the God of Christians in human history. They validate and complement one another.

The extensive literature on myth cannot be ignored by liturgists and sacramental theologians. It is important in understanding the nature and function of biblical readings in the liturgy, and significant in grasping the character and rôle of liturgical preaching, the structure and meaning of the feasts and seasons of the Church year, and the place of the sacraments in celebrating the life of individuals and communities. It must be noted, however, that anthropologists who choose to comment on the place of myth in the life of Christians have to be aware of the incarnational principle which is basic in Christianity. The divine has become immanent in humanity in the life and person of Jesus Christ so that humanity might share in the very transcendence of the divine.

Like myth, ritual is a constitutive element in every religion. Since it can be observed and described, ritual is more readily understood than myth, at least on a surface level. As patterned, repetitive, formal behaviour, ritual is either secular or religious. When it is religious, it attempts to relate human persons to the sacred. Among anthropologists, great stress is placed on its stereotyped, formal, standardized character. Hence ritual is sometimes identified with ceremony.

Anthropological studies have generally stressed the various functions which rituals perform in the total life of a culture. From a religious point of view they reinforce religious beliefs and enable people to relate to the spiritual world. By engaging in religious rituals, participants acquire a sense of identity with a religious body or sect. They also internalize a sense of the religious values upheld by the group.

These anthropological insights have severe limitations for Christians. Christian liturgy has much in common with ritual but the two must not be equated. Christian liturgy is a celebration of a mystery which is not only past but present and future. It is not only a remembrance of what has occurred but the celebration of what occurs here and now in the liturgy itself. Likewise it includes an expectation of what is yet to come. Hence the formal, repetitive aspect of liturgy must make allowance for a spontaneous, creative dimension. The God whom Christians relate to is a creator God. By sharing in his life, they also share in his ability to create and to transform what has already been created. Furthermore the purpose of Christian liturgy is not only to constitute the community of the Church but also to promote the development of unique persons within the Church.

The distinguished American anthropologist, Margaret Mead, has written a very helpful essay on celebration which takes account of the programmed and spontaneous aspects of ritual.[14] Her insights are especially useful to liturgists. While reacting negatively to the superficiality of modern 'happenings', she stresses the need for a proper balance between the old and the new in human celebrations. She notes that when rituals are too rich and the highly elaborated symbolism too old to be appropriate to contemporary life, people are apt to be overwhelmed, detached, alienated, and apathetic. Likewise, when the symbol system is too shallow, people's lives are apt to be deprived and their experience tends to be superficial. These insights are especially useful at the present time of liturgical renewal.

Although there is great stress on symbolism in contemporary philosophy, psychology, literature, art, and theology, most modern textbooks in anthropology do not give it an important place. Some anthropologists stress its significance in expressing and constituting human relationships with the divine, but their studies are not based on a uniform definition of symbol and their conclusions vary considerably. Their concern is usually with the function of symbols rather than the inner meaning expressed. Obviously, then, the literature at its present stage of development is of very limited use to liturgists and sacramental theologians.

CONCLUSIONS

At the beginning of this paper it was noted that a revisionist model of theology would seem to provide an effective method whereby the traditional expressions of Christian faith and common human experience can be correlated with one another. The method is basically interdisciplinary. Special difficulties arise, however, in an effort to relate contemporary anthropology to Christian theology, especially liturgical theology, since there are serious shortcomings in the anthropological studies of religion. Nevertheless, the discipline does raise important questions about the nature of religion and its relation to human life in general. These are issues that affect liturgical theology and practice. However, primitive ritual and Catholic liturgy are comparable only to a limited extent. It would seem imperative that liturgists who attempt to implement the insights of anthropologists should acquire a thorough grounding in anthropology if they are to avoid the pitfalls of naïveté and superficiality. Likewise, anthropologists who attempt to criticize liturgical celebrations and the experience of those who participate need adequate training in and understanding of Christology, ecclesiology, sacramental theology and Christian anthropology. The demands on those who pursue the revisionist model of theology are certainly great, but that model would seem to be especially adequate for theology's task at the present time.

Notes

1. The most adequate exposition of this method is found in David Tracy, *Blessed Rage for Order* (New York, 1975).

2. *Gaudium et Spes,* n. 25: *AAS* 58 (1966), p. 1045.

3. *Sacrosanctum Concilium,* nn. 37–40: *AAS* (1964), pp. 110–11.

4. *GS,* nn. 40, 44: *AAS* 58 (1966), pp. 1057–58, 1064.

5. Cf. Peter Coughlin, 'The New Order of the Mass', in *Chicago Studies,* 16 (1977), p. 77.

6. Ibid.

7. *GS,* nn. 53–62: *AAS* 58 (1966), pp. 1075–84.

8. 'Religion and the Anthropologists', in E. E. Evans-Pritchard, *Social Anthropology and Other Essays* (New York, 1964), p. 153.

9. For a survey of anthropological literature on religion, I acknowledge my indebtedness to an unpublished paper by John A. Saliba, 'Religion and the Anthropologists: 1960–1976'.

10. Cf. Robert N. Bellah, 'Religion in the University: Changing Consciousness: Changing Structures', in *Religion in the Undergraduate Curriculum,* ed. Claude Welch (Washington, D.C., 1972), p. 14.

11. Ibid.

12. (New York, 1974), p. 319.

13. Cf. James Hitchcock, *The Recovery of the Sacred* (New York, 1974).

14. 'Celebration: A Human Need', in Margaret Mead, *Twentieth Century Faith: Hope and Survival* (New York, 1972), pp. 123–30.

Aidan Kavanagh

Life-Cycle Events,
Civil Ritual and the Christian

THE PROBLEM STATED

ANTHROPOLOGICAL and psychological research in recent decades has shed significant light on the social, symbolic, and religious implications of human life-cycle events and civil ritual.[1] Among other things, these studies suggest not only how normal and, indeed, inevitable the conformation of Christian liturgical patterns within these cultural structures is, but also how complex is the process, and how vast are its implications for Christian theory and practice.

Perhaps even more importantly, however, the same studies affirm *Peter Berger's* observation that '*society* is the guardian of order and meaning not only objectively, in its institutional structure, but subjectively as well, in its structuring of individual consciousness'.[2] In this milieu the Church lives, pervading it at times, in opposition to it at others, but in some degree of tension with it always. The Gospel abides, but the world provides the modes by which it is proclaimed and lived. Needless to say this is hardly good news to Christian sectarians, be they orthodox monastics, curial elitists, or biblical fundamentalists. To complicate things further, it is a datum of classic theology that God works on both sides of the Christianity-culture equation. As my colleague, *William Muehl,* expresses it: 'There are social values . . . which may reflect the divine will at a given moment more fully than competing religious claims, and these must be protected against ecclesiastical presumptions'.[3]

The positions of Berger and Muehl are, additionally, socio-cultural specifications of the standard teaching that God is not bound to the sacramental order; that while the Church gives sure and certain access to God, he is not the Church's exclusive 'property' because he is creator of all things, as his incarnate Son is saviour of all. The Son has become not merely an ecclesiastical Personage or a sacramental captive, but the sole cosmic redemptive force pervading and outstripping all human cultures. Thus, when Berger and Muehl insist upon respect for the integrity of extraecclesial society, they are stating a tension that lies deep in the tradition of Judaeo-Christian theology. They are not merely singing the praises of the secular city, nor are they suggesting that the Gospel must sit at the world's knee to learn God's mind.

I say all this at the outset because it is easy for Christians to react to crucial events in the human life-cycle or in the civil arena by withdrawing from them altogether, as though these events have nothing to do with the Gospel or the churches. While it may be possible for individuals or specific groups to live a Christian life for a time abstracted from events of the human life-cycle and civil religion, as it has come to be called, it may seriously be doubted whether that life can be sustained indefinitely in such a manner. The history of liturgical evolution in both East and West suggests the contrary: it also makes unmistakeably clear that the most compelling ritual complexes emerge out of popular consciousness formed by a symbiosis of Gospel and world. The feast of Christmas is but one example, that amalgam of pagan cult, solar equinox, ending of the civil year, and Christian celebration of the mystery of the incarnation. (In this connexion, as a professional ecclesiastic, I might perhaps confess a reserve over the singing of 'Happy Birthday Dear Jesus' at Christmas Mass in my parish similar to that of Leo the Great over people's bowing to the rising sun before entering the Vatican basilica for the same Mass in the fifth century.[4] I doubt that Leo prevailed: I am sure I shall not.)

RISKS OF COMPROMISE

At the same time, it is just as easy for Christians to succumb to crucial events in the human life-cycle or in the arena of civil religion, compromising the Gospel as they do so. This is perhaps more the temptation of our own era than the former option of withdrawal. One hears much about the need to adapt the liturgy to cultural needs, to produce new symbols to make the sacraments relevant to modern experience. The more crude attempts to do these things are obvious and need not detain us here. But certain past attempts to do the same thing, attempts which have received the sanction of time and convention, if not of tradition, are more difficult to deal with. Some of them deserve our attention, at least in passing.

Most notably in the area of Christian initiation, there can be little doubt that conventionally relating baptism and confirmation to the life-cycle events of birth and maturity produces a host of difficulties in attaining an adequate grasp of what these two sacraments truly are. The analogies of baptism with physical birth and of confirmation with personal maturity or social majority have become practical univocities that require baptism to be treated as the special sacrament of early infancy and confirmation correlatively as the special sacrament of adolescence. This assumption having become entrenched leads into an imperceptible transfer of one's own personal public confession of Christian faith from baptism to confirmation. It leaves baptism as little more than a preliminary if major exorcism of sin, and inflates confirmation into a *de facto* surrogate baptism administered in the midst of adolescent socio-psychic individuation crises. Moreover, as the sacraments of penance and eucharist are inserted between baptism in infancy and confirmation in adolescence, the intelligibility of the initiatory process breaks down even further: baptism-penance-eucharist become events preludic to full interior and exterior confession of faith and public acceptance into the Church in confirmation.

It is beyond the scope of this essay to unravel the history of this development or to list the inconveniences it is causing in catechetical formation, sacramental coherence, and pastoral practice. It must suffice only to cite it as a major example of what happens when the faith community perceives only the samenesses that are half and forgets the differences that constitute the other half of any analogy. For baptism is indeed about birth, but it is not about birth in the natural order. Even less is it merely a rite of passage into civil enfranchisement. There is nothing intrinsically infantile about Christian baptism, nor is there anything intrinsically adolescent about confirmation. In a similar way, one should emphasize that the sacrament of holy orders is not about designating persons for civic or ethnic leadership; the sacrament of matrimony is not about giving sanction to romantic love; the sacrament of anointing is not about cures of physical ills that physicians will not or cannot cure. Nor is the eucharist only a celebration of life or a genteel Christian ritual of euphoria, an ecumenical tea-service correlative without qualification to the well-known hospitality ritual of Chinese culture.

METHOD OF LITURGICAL REFORM

When these crucial differences are forgotten, past assumptions begin to merge with modern misapprehensions concerning what, for lack of a better phrase, I shall call the methodology of liturgical reform. Of first importance here is the necessity of recalling just how unprecedented the recent process of liturgical reform in the western Church has been. As *Robert Taft* has pointed out, what has been done with the western liturgy in the last twenty years has no parallel in the history of religions: '. . . representatives sat down in committee and decided to change the ritual pattern of a whole people's way of relating to God'.[5] The committee process, as careful as it has been, has inevitably given rise to organizational and research attitudes that have affected the results dramatically. One such attitude is that of structural-functionalism, borrowed from the social sciences. This attitude leads to experts manipulating structures such as sacraments and their liturgical enactment so as to enhance, modify, or redirect their functions for the good of those using the structures. Thus not only were the people using the structures largely ignored, and their 'good' sometimes seriously misdiagnosed, but the long, slow, and complex evolutionary process that has always been typical of crucial human patterns such as language and liturgy was drastically reduced to less than two decades.

Another attitude, which has begun to come to the fore more recently, has been characterized by *John Grabner* as one of 'relentless ritual rationalism'. [6] This attitude first analyzes ritual phenomena at large, then it compares its analysis to Christian liturgical patterns in specific, and concludes with a critique of the Christian patterns controlled by anthropological data resulting from its analysis of ritual phenomena at large. As one who has long urged liturgical scholars to take such data into account while maintaining the usual historical and theological methods followed in the past, and as one who has taught a regular course over the past ten years entitled 'Anthropology of Ritual Behaviour', I may perhaps be allowed to make two criticisms of this second attitude. First, the 'anthropology' practised by recent adherents to this attitude often leaves much to be desired. Liturgists and pastors usually know 'anthropology' in a very spotty and uneven way: almost none of them are prepared to practice its demanding, complex, and difficult methodology, especially in interpreting its data. Second, anthropologists themselves just as often know little about liturgical history and even less about theology. As an example of what often occurs when anthropological amateurs on the one hand and theological and liturgical amateurs on the other hand join forces, a Christian sacrament such as confirmation is transmuted into a modern social or civil *rite de passage* in much the same way scholastic theologians without access to the data of liturgical history turned confirmation into a medieval rite of majority, and as polemicists at the time of the Reformation turned it into an ordinance or sacrament of Christian education nor dissimilar from a graduation ceremony at the end of a curriculum of ecclesiastical instruction. In none of these three cases is the original baptismal context of chrismation-handlaying invoked as a datum *intrinsic* to confirmational interpretation and practice. It cannot be emphasized too strongly that this error in method, which may seem insignificant to many, has enormous results not only for confirmation in itself but for the whole of the sacramental order—if the latter is indeed not merely a series of independent ritual acts but an economy of intimately related events in which the Word made flesh becomes act and *praxis*. No amount of anthropological data can account for the intent of confirmation, as related to baptism, to signify '. . . the unity of the paschal mystery, the close relationship between the mission of the Son and the pouring out of the Holy Spirit, and the joint celebration of the sacraments by which the Son and the Spirit come with the Father upon those who are baptized'. [7]

RITUAL AND HUMAN LIFE

My intent is not to dismiss professional reflection upon anthropological data so far as Christian worship is concerned. Even less is it to exalt the historian and theologian as the only ones who can instruct us on the liturgy's meaning. My point is, however, to encourage more sophisticated discrimination in the way differing types of data and interpretative methodologies are used when they are brought to bear on Christian worship patterns. Unexamined assumptions, furthermore, must not be allowed to filter out data that are perceived to be, at least unconsciously, inconvenient. 'Could it be', asks *Aelred Tegels,* for example, 'that the prescription of the Sacred Constitution [*sic*] on the Liturgy (34), that "the rites should be distinguished by a noble simplicity, that they should be short, clear, and free from useless repetitions" runs contrary to basic anthropological findings concerning human ritual behaviour?' [8] Those findings are in fact complementary to the results of ordinary reflection upon the quality of 'noble simplicity' itself: namely, that while clarity is always a function of it, brevity rarely is, and rhythmic repetition is most often an intimate component of it. When people assemble to enact values they consider to be of crucial importance to their own survival, their efforts may well be nobly simple and usually are; but they are rarely brief, and they are highly repetitious. Initiation into social majority among modern civilized societies takes decades, not weeks: the 'consecration' of a modern head of state takes months if not years, and his or her inauguration takes days, not minutes. Christians pauperize their sacraments if they reduce them to momentary confections, thereby attaining not 'noble simplicity' but only sporadic, a-rhythmic blandness.

For any ritual, liturgical or otherwise, is more than a communication code. It is also what *Victor Turner* calls '. . . a synchronization of many performative genres . . . often ordered by a dramatic structure, which energizes and gives emotional coloring to the interdependent communicative codes which express in manifold ways the meaning of the leitmotif'.[9] Ritual involves not just one's mind but the senses and emotions simultaneously, modulating all these by kinaesthetic (dance and gesture) and sonic media.

Because of the crucial nature of the values it evokes and reenforces, ritual rises to the level of paradigm—anticipating change as well as inscribing order in the minds and hearts of its participants. In this, '. . . the deepest meaning people have come to assign to key features of personal and social experience' is focused upon the total person in the total culture.[10]

CHRISTIAN LITURGY AND CIVIL RITUAL

Five-minute homilies and thirty-minute masses devoted to 'themes' such as love or social justice may sometimes accomplish all this, but as a rule they do not. By itself, this is perhaps one reason why communities of Christians liturgically so undernourished find themselves overpowered by the awesome vigor of popular civil rituals, of a secular aesthetic intensified in the entertainment media, and of the singular meaning one discovers for oneself in the life-crises of birth-puberty-death. Unable to compete with these, such a Christian community may attempt to withdraw into itself, becoming de facto sectarian religiously and ghettoized culturally: or it may attempt to adapt its own thin ritual structure to the robust cultural patterns it finds around it, thus foregoing its own internal sense of cohesion and identity. Should it do the first of these, it will have forgotten that God is not bound to reveal himself only within the community. Should it do the second of these, it will have forgotten that the world, however robust its cultural patterns may seem, stands nonetheless under God's judgment, and that, while he may indeed reveal himself outside the Church, sure and certain access to him is had only from within it. In either case, the pathological element lies not in the awesome vigour of civil rituals, a secular aesthetic, and the singular meaning of an individual's life-crises, but in the liturgical undernourishment to which the Christian group has become accustomed.

Two related principles must be invoked in order to correct this situation. First, the Christian group must understand that adequate liturgical nourishment for itself cannot be achieved exclusively from its own resources. Neither the Hebrew Bible nor Christian Scriptures have much to say about life-crises; Jesus himself said nothing that survives about puberty. Civil religion is assumed as something that exists and is unavoidable ('Render unto Caesar those things that are Caesar's . . .'), and a secular aesthetic in our modern sense did not exist. The point here is that the scripture-based tradition does not regard the Judaeo-Christian community as sustaining its own appropriate identity from era to era over against a context wholly external to itself: the criteria for this are rather to be found in God's own revelation of himself and in the community's faithful response thereunto: that is, in a bilateral covenant-relationship of which the creator is the source. While the source is transcultural, the recipient community is not: it hears the Word in place and time, with accent and idiom, and it keeps the covenant by *praxis* in the same manner. To worship in spirit and in truth can thus never mean worshipping abstractly. This is what the iconoclastic controversy was about, and it remains to the credit of Byzantine theologians that they perceived the issue as an aesthetic one having everything to do with an adequate doctrine of the Word *incarnate*. An orthodox *iconodule* no doubt would have regarded abstract worship as a monophysitic denial of Christ's humanity just as much as he would have regarded worship reduced to a purely didactic or aesthetic melange of 'cultural' ceremonies as an Arian denial of Jesus' divinity. Orthodoxy is served only by keeping the two extremes in vital tension—a tension that is wholly necessary if one is to see the incarnation of the Word not as a mere catechetical condescension to human weakness, but as an act worthy of God because rooted in the very nature of the Trinity itself from before always.[11]

The implacable theandrism of the Christian community's covenant-relationship means that its worship, while radically theocentric, deploys itself in human accents, cultural idioms, and finite rhythms. Being mutable, these must be constantly passed beneath the judgment of the Gospel, but they are in no way dispensable in the *praxis* of faith. And while no enfleshment, divine or ecclesial, is without risk, not every risk need be morbid unless the community allows it to become so. Refusing to risk cultural engagement may be fatal indeed, since it assures that the community's liturgical nourishment will become or remain less than adequate.

The second principle is implicit in the first. It is that too great a self-consciousness on the part of a Christian group concerning what accents, idioms, and rhythms it ingests from the culture surrounding it, or too great an artificiality in the process by which this is accomplished, can render the results sterile for the community's own life. One of the matters we know least about in liturgical history is how the detailed evolution of rites took place during and immediately after periods of significant cultural shift: for example, from a Semitic to a Hellenistic milieu or from a classical Mediterranean to a European medieval one. More often than not, the evidence that survives indicates clearly that the shift occurred, but few if any details of how it happened are given.

Although sporadic evidence of resistance to certain changes exists—as with Jerome for example—one is left with the distinct impression that ingestion of cultural patterns into church polity and worship was regarded in general as unavoidable, unremarkable, normal, and for the most part healthy. Few bishops seem to have exerted special efforts to give structure to the process in a formal way, and some who did have left their names forever attached to their churches' liturgies to this day—such as Basil and John Chrysostom in the East and Ambrose and Gregory in the West. Yet even the work of these has about it less the character of creative innovation and more that of editorial sifting and standardization after the fact.

For symbols are carried in the vital pulses and structures of a social group. They may be discovered: they may mutate. But they can never be confected by a committee out of whole cloth. They may sometimes be transplanted, once discovered, from one social life-system to another, but this does not always work, and its doing is never a simple or an easy matter. When we speak of 'adapting the liturgy' to modern cultures, one suspects that the truth of the process is to be found rather in such a transplantation of cultural symbols *into* the liturgy than in suddenly conforming the liturgy to symbolic patterns detected in cultures. The process is then found to be less manipulative of the liturgy (as one might adjust a machine) and more ingestive and symbiotic (as the growth of an organism that has been cross-fertilized with a sympathetic species). The latter process is so imperceptible in the life-span of individuals as to escape comment. It is more similar to slow and steady organic growth than to sudden mechanical adjustment.

It is easy enough to cite examples of what happens to the deep if delicate web of human relationships when the 'organic' nature of their origin, maintenance, and evolution is over-ridden by recourse to mechanical manipulation. City planners who wish to benefit urban areas by efficient, cost-conscious means so as to enhance traffic patterns, commerce, and the landscape often do so by destroying that most fragile of urban phenomena, a human neighbourhood. What took generations to evolve is quickly obliterated, changed into grids of architecture and open spaces in which people find it difficult to initiate, support, and develop humane relationships. When these roots vanish, a crucial area of social tissue dies, and what has made the *polis* or *civitas* perhaps the primary corporate human artifact is rendered inaccessible.

Septic human relationships cannot survive in an antiseptic bath of psycho-social formaldehyde. Those relationships are articulated not only in time and space but in patterns of activity such as ritual as well. So far as the liturgical life of a Christian community is concerned, it is well to recall the analogy of the organism especially at times when cultural shift is as rapid and wrenching as it seems to be today. *Alvin Toffler,* examining the psycho-social damage done by rapid change, could just as well be speaking of Christian liturgy as of civic ritual when he writes: '. . . Repetitive behaviour, whatever else its functions, helps give meaning to non-repetitive events by providing the backdrop against which novelty is silhouetted'.[12] He even suggests that 'As we accelerate and introduce a-rhythmic patterns into the pace of change, we need to mark off certain regularities for preservation', rather as we designate forests, national monuments, or animal sanctuaries for protection. He errs, however, as social behaviorists often do, when he concludes: 'We may even need to *manufacture* ritual'.[13]

CONCLUSION

If a Christian group is to correct its liturgical undernourishment by ingesting cultural elements patiently into its own *praxis* of convenant-faith in God through Christ, it must do so in the knowledge that, when it deals with symbolic patterns, not all these need be rendered overtly Christian in order to function for the group's good. Symbols abroad in a culture are unavoidable and thus always functional to some degree. To be blunt about it, if there are functioning puberty rites or ceremonies of civil majority present in a given culture, there seems little reason why these have to be reproduced *within* the Christian community's sacramental-liturgical system. Rather, a more healthy polity might seek to take advantage of such external patterns simply by overrunning them with faithful Christians who, in passing regularly through them, steadily purify them of connotations inimical to the Gospel and instil in them a sense of the creator's intent for all creation, human or otherwise.

In this view, the need to adapt confirmation to cultural rites of puberty, majority, or even of refreshment or 'renewal', might free the sacrament to return to its wholly authentic and rather modest rôle as the public sealing in the Holy Spirit of baptism. In this view, overcoming the need to sustain baptism as a birth sacrament fixed in infancy, in recognition of cultural needs to announce and have recognized a new birth, might free the sacrament to return to its wholly authentic and crucial rôle as the articulator of evangelization, catechesis, pastoral care, and even eucharistic celebration. For the eucharist begins in baptism, and baptism is sustained in the *eucharistia* of a Spirit-filled Church.

Manipulating baptism and confirmation so as to conform them to life-cycle events or civil rituals that are perceived as somehow laden with a power more relevant to 'successful' Christian living than these

sacraments' own inherent power and meaning is a questionable enterprise. The power of these events and rituals is without question: they
are also best left to function in their own proper context, with their
results in the lives of Christians who encounter them purified and
strengthened by the faith and *praxis* found in vigorous rhythms of the
sacrament order and the robust nourishment of liturgical life.

To conclude with an illustration of how modestly robust the Christian initiatory pattern really is, I submit that the data of tradition on
confirmation represent a sort of fundamental equation from which one
cannot depart, but which, at the same time, must be refactored and
appropriated anew in each generation. The results may never be identi-
cal, but they will nonetheless always be faithful to the Gospel as lived
in act and *praxis*. The data are fourfold.

First, a sealing in the Spirit is included within the total baptismal
synaxis at least by the early third century if not during the course of the
second.

Second, this sealing occurs in direct, intimate, and inseparable relationship with the Spirit-filled water-event; and *with* that water-event,
plus the Spirit-filled table-event of eucharistic thanksgiving, constitutes
baptism-in-its-fullness.

Third, the form the sealing takes is that of an oleagenous hand-laying
and consignation, with epicletic prayer.

And fourth, the form, place, and meaning of the sealing have abso-
lutely nothing to do with the physical *or* social *or* emotional *or* intellectual *or* even spiritual 'age' of the initiate. The form, place, and meaning
of the sealing have rather to do with the fact that the initiate is entering
fully into the community of faith through the passion, death, and resurrection of Christ, who has himself become the 'life-giving Spirit' by
which the community believes and lives.

There is a certain 'noble simplicity' here that is quite modestly clear.
But no one who has ever come to this faith, or assisted anyone else to
come to it, can doubt that the process is long, hard, and anything but
brief and easy. This we all know: what we often forget, however, is
that when this is said it is referred not only (perhaps not even primarily)
to the individual initiate, but to the Church which initiates and is being
entered into. Because the Spirit groans in the Church, the individual
initiate finds him or herself filled with unspeakable groanings. The rite
of initiation *sacramentalizes* a person's own unique and, otherwise,
barely communicable conversion in faith. The rite *ecclesializes* that
conversion in faith, taking the convert out of the private sector definitively and making him or her a radically public person of the Church
universal and local, a *fidelis,* one who is now empowered by the Spirit
to sustain the Word become flesh in act and *praxis*.

Notes

1. See, for example, A. van Gennep, *The Rites of Passage*, (1908) trans. M. B. Vizedom and G. L. Caffee (Chicago, 1960); E. Erikson, Ontogeny of Ritualization in Man, *Philosophical Transactions of the Royal Society of London*, Series B, 251 (1966) 337–350; V. Turner, *The Forest of Symbols: Aspects of Ndembu Ritual* (Ithaca, N. Y., 1967) and *The Ritual Process: Structure and Anti-Structure* (Chicago, 1969); Mary Douglas, *Natural Symbols: Explorations in Cosmology* (London & New York, 1970). Also *The Roots of Ritual*, ed. James D. Shaughnessy (Grand Rapids, Michigan, 1973)—a collection of essays by anthropologists, theologians, liturgical scholars, and cultural critics reviewing the literature exemplified by the above titles.

2. *The Sacred Canopy* (New York, 1967), p. 21. Emphasis added.

3. 'Long Live the King', *Reflection* (Yale Divinity School Journal) 74, (January 1977), p. 2.

4. Sermon XXVII in *A Select Library of Nicene and Post-Nicene Fathers, etc.*, ed. P. Schaff and H. Wace, 12 (1894), p. 140.

5. Interview in *Hucusque*, the bulletin of the Murphy Center for Liturgical Research, University of Notre Dame, Notre Dame, Indiana 3 (November 1976), no pagination.

6. 'Ritual for a New Day', *Hucusque* 4 (April 1977), no pagination.

7. The Latin of the *Ordo Initiationis Christianae Adultorum*, paragraph 34, is even more clear and forceful: *Hac connexione significantur unitas mysterii paschalis, necessitudo inter missionem Filii et effusionem Spiritus Sancti coniunctioque sacramentorum quibus utraque persona divina cum Patre baptizatis advenit.*

8. 'Chronicle', *Worship* 50 (1976), p. 539.

9. 'Ritual, Tribal and Catholic', *Worship* 50 (1976), p. 505.

10. Ibid., p. 506.

11. See Otto Demus, *Byzantine Mosaic Decoration: Aspects of Monumental Art in Byzantium* (1948; New York, 1976), pp. 5–6.

12. *Future Shock* (New York, 1970), p. 394.

13. Ibid., p. 395. Emphasis added.

Joachim Scharfenberg

Human Maturation and Christian Symbols

A TRUE rapprochement between Christian theology and the humanities is, to this day, hard to achieve. For a scholar working in the
humanities, 'the Galileo case' remains traumatic and religion is still
viewed, as it was by Freud, as the great adversary in the struggle
towards progress and human development. Theologians see the
humanities as 'the great threat' and feel driven to wage a 'running
battle' in an attempt to define their true area of concern, so that for a
long time, as clear a division as possible between the two disciplines
has seemed to be in the interests of both parties. It is, however, easy to
show that where a dialogue between theology and the humanities has
taken place, it has proved advantageous to both sides. In this context, I
should like to try to show how fruitful a dialogue can be: both for the
development of the concept of maturation and for the understanding of
the Christian pronouncement, which is to a great extent expressed
symbolically.

CRITIQUE OF RELIGION: THE IMPUTATION OF IMMATURITY

The classic critiques of religion of Feuerbach, Nietzsche or Marx,
which either try to reduce religion to 'the little man's' desire for com-
pensation for his inferiority, or to 'false consciousness', are to this
extent in agreement: religion does not accord with the level of maturity
of grown men and women; rather it seeks to manipulate and exploit
them by artificially maintaining and prolonging their childish projections and emotional world with the false consolations of heaven. Sig-

mund Freud, who simply wanted to provide a psychological foundation [1] for the critique of religion of his great philosophical forbears, coined the later famous dictum: religion is the 'regressive revival of the forces that protected our infancy'; [2] it is an emphatically childish attempt to handle 'the real world in which we are placed, by means of the world of our projections'. [3] Religion seemed to him to make everything as we would like it to be [4] and he thus regarded it as a temptation that must be resisted: 'man cannot remain a child forever'. [5] 'Experience teaches us: the world is not a nursery'. [6] The rejection of religion must coincide inexorably with the process of growth; man cannot cling to illusions but must come to terms with reality. [7] Among the theologians who have taken this challenge seriously, I shall consider first the Zürich Protestant pastor, Oskar Pfister, who saw psychoanalysis as the ideal means of freeing the Christian faith 'from the dross of the Oedipus complex', [8] and who sought to employ the potentially valuable insights of psychoanalysis to enhance our understanding of religion. With sure instinct he recognized the weakness of the Freudian concept of maturation as amounting to nothing more than a 'judicious resignation' with which we must learn submissively to bear the great inevitabilities of fate. 'Who is telling me that submission should be the last word? Why should it be?' [9] he protested. But above all it was the Anglican theologian R. S. Lee whose discriminating dialogue with psychoanalysis brought him to the insight that even the Christian faith is historically conditioned and that its central task consists in the continuing attempt to liberate it and cleanse it from non-Christian elements. [10] His decisive question was therefore: 'Is Christianity the expression of a free ego, dependent on the reality principle and based on a real knowledge of the world; or is it a product of the unconscious, springing from fantasies and only selecting and using such knowledge as it needs to further its unconscious wishes?' [11] Lee makes maturation the central concept in his critique of religion and indeed he does so not without a critical use of Freud's own conception. Very ingeniously, he demonstrates that even the atheism that Freud wished to represent could reflect a level of immaturity: namely, the projection of the desire to be rid of the father, but where, unconsciously, in some form or other, the wish for a father creeps in again, giving even atheism the appearance of a number of totalitarian and authoritarian systems. [12] In a second work, Lee tries to show that an encounter with the Christian symbols in the liturgy must be regarded as a very real aid to maturation. The principal aspects which he examines are: 'the activity of the whole personality' [13] which can limit the damaging separation of conscious from unconscious striving; the 'development of the self' and the 'basic impulses of personality'; [14] and finally the finding of the self and the growth to maturity which are the preconditions for the finding of God.[15]

Here at last the question arises: what must be understood by human maturity? Among the critics of religion who have made this concept the criterion of the religious phenomenon, 'the way to supermen' is, next to Freud's 'judicious resignation', formulated as the projected aim. But in the course of history, this has itself been discredited, or is but the prescription of juvenile revolutionary protest, which frequently relinquishes the ideal of maturation and seeks to maintain recourse to and perpetuation of infantile emotions and desires. Among scholars in the humanities, Erik H. Erikson seems to me to have come nearest to a reformulation of the concept of maturation. As a professional 'frontier-crosser' [16] he has deliberately ignored the divisions between disciplines and has transcended the boundary that was traditionally believed to separate theology from the humanities.

A CONTRIBUTION TOWARDS A REFORMULATION OF THE CONCEPT OF MATURATION

In that Erikson links the concept of maturation and the question of his own identity, he deliberately makes his own central conflict (and manifestly that of his entire generation!) the principal theme of his life's work. He had himself had to experience and come to terms with the revelation that those agencies and institutions, that into our own century, had been the foundation and guarantee of identity, were themselves fragile: above all, the family, the nation, the profession, and religion.

(a) Erikson was born near Frankfurt on 15 July 1902, the child of a Danish artist then living in Germany. His parents had separated before his birth. Because of an illness, which he himself later described as 'an illness from the absence of his father', his mother met a Jewish paediatrician, Dr Homburger, whom she later married and who adopted the little Erik. For a long time, throughout his childhood and adolescence, the fact of his adoption was concealed from him, and it was only as a man of over thirty-five that he took his real father's surname and relegated that of his stepfather to the position of the 'American middlename'.

(b) A Dane by birth, Erikson grew up bilingual and attended a German secondary school that specialized in classics and the humanities. Having studied psychoanalysis in Vienna from 1927–33 he inevitably came to realize, when he and his Canadian wife fled from the Nazis, that he would no longer be at home in his native Denmark. He emigrated to the United States, learned English with great difficulty and as a man of over thirty, began to work, think and write in it. During the

McCarthy era in the nineteen-fifties, he declined to sign the oath of allegiance and lost the professorship at the University of Berkeley to which he had only recently been appointed. An American, approaching fifty years old, he was told to go back where he had come from.[17]

(c) Erikson had only found a professional identity with great difficulty. After the school-leaving examination, he had spent a year wandering irresolutely with a rucksack on his back in the Black Forest and the area around Lake Constance. He experienced what he was himself to call a 'psychosocial moratorium'. Identification with his childhood may have been what caused him to decide to become an art teacher. He even worked in a school but immediately accepted an offer from Anna Freud to study psychoanalysis with her 'for at that time psychoanalysis drew mainly those who didn't quite belong anywhere else'.[18] Here he acquired a training as close to that of a paediatrician as was possible without studying medicine. He put up with a professional life which forced him to work in institutions and areas for which he was not formally qualified. The American Psychoanalytical Association, which had by then decided to accept only medical doctors, gave him a special status.

(d) Even in the field of religion, Erikson proved himself to be a 'professional frontier-crosser'. During World War I, his school fellows taunted him with his Jewishness while at the same time this withdrawn, blond, blue-eyed boy was known as 'the Goy' in the synagogue where he was taken by his strictly orthodox parents. Later he exemplified essential aspects of his concept of identity in his treatment of the hero of Protestantism, Martin Luther, and in his book on Gandhi as a representative of far-eastern spirituality, which was almost totally ignored by the classical psychoanalytical psychology of religion. In his 'ontogenesis of ritualization' [19] he arrives at a kind of vindication of ritually determined forms of piety, and in *Toys and Reasons* he directs his analysis to the ritualisation of experience.[20]

Such a crisis of identity and maturation, existentially experienced and endured, demanded something that Jürgen Habermas once called the 'general interpretation' which insists that the narrative form should be retained but the historical proscription broken: 'It has the form of a narrative because it is to aid subjects in reconstructing their own life history in narrative form. But it can serve as the background of many such narrations only because it does not hold merely for an individual case'.[21] It is my impression that Erikson met with the demand for a 'general interpretation' in an exemplary way. He recounted the problems and conflicts that lie in the area of the problematic of maturation and identity more vividly than he deduced them in an abstract way. But what was Erikson trying to do when he gave a predominantly narrative character to his concept of identity? Primarily, he wanted to portray the 'connexion between the individual and history',[22] which amounted to nothing less than a study of typical identity crises in various historical periods (and among different groups within the same period), so as to construct a model that would prove to be 'no less an historical than a clinical tool'.[23]

Thus the old and frequently reiterated question of whether the gains in knowledge in the depth psychology of individuals can be transferred to collective and historical phenomena, is exposed as fallacious. In his work on maturity and identity, Erikson searches for a hermeneutical key which will afford a better understanding not only of the people with whom he is concerned but of history.

This brings us up against the central question in the construction of a theory of pastoral theology. For if I fail to succeed in understanding the conflicts of the people with whom I am concerned, and fail in my understanding of the Christian tradition, which I should like to apply to the resolution of these conflicts by means of the same hermeneutical key, then pastoral care and communication inevitably become a matter of doctrine. We must therefore consider whether a reformulation of the concept of maturation, on the lines of Erikson's reformulation of the concept of identity, can adequately serve as such a hermeneutical key. That this, in view of the self-interpretation of people today, is the case, seems to me to be unquestionable. But whether this key can also bring us to a better understanding of the symbols of the Christian tradition, remains to be illustrated.

THE CONCEPT OF IDENTITY AS A HERMENEUTICAL KEY TO CHRISTIAN SYMBOLS

In that Erikson juxtaposes the mature ethics of adults, with infantile morals and juvenile ideology [24]—an opposition which holds not just for individuals but for the whole of humanity in its progress through history—, he constructs a normative image of man. His work aims to contribute something of significance in the form of a new kind of humanness, a humanity where acuity keeps pace with capacity for action, where activity keeps pace with unrestricted thought. He poses not just the question of what kind of humanity we are moving towards, but that of what kind of people we should be, if we are to handle the problems posed by the future. He can thus be regarded as an early practitioner of futurology, of research into the future. He considers fast and continuous social change to be a problem that should be met by psychoanalytical theory. And in this context ego-function assumes an increased significance: the ego is no longer a weak, helpless thing, harassed and subjugated, the helpless rider of a wild horse; rather its fundamental virtues are: confidence, will, singleness of purpose, industriousness, loyalty and reliability, love, caring and wisdom. 'For the only alternative to armed competition seems to be to activate in the historical partner what will strengthen him in his historical development even as it strengthens the actor in his own development toward a common future identity'.[25] Thus Erikson has become by necessity a critic of culture, which means not simply that man must accommodate himself to his environment but also that the world must be adapted to the epigenetic potentialities of man. His concept of identity brings him to the conclusion that there are societies which have become so heterogeneous and disorganized and which change so rapidly, that they no longer offer a child growing up in them the essential support, through consistency and recognition, that is so necessary. Against this background of the interrelation of social structure and character-type, Erikson demands of the future a new type of human being: 'generative man'.[26] 'Generativity is primarily the interest in the persuasion and education of the next generation' and the relevant quality is 'care for things and for people'.[27]

Thus the notion of identity is related to the generation cycle and tries to capture the whole range of biological, psychological, social and cultural elements which place men in the context of what preceded them and what will come after them. In a sense this can be seen as a logical reversal of traditional psychological development psychology. It is not origin that determines the steps towards progress and development, these are not a sublimation of what came earlier, but rather the aim and purpose of humanity is teleologically determined. This is defined as 'care of others' and is, as a virtue, the result as much of biological necessity as of free human endeavour. It is therefore a synthesis that is aspired to, or in the terminology of Ernst Bloch: the symbol of an actual utopia.

If I may summarize Erikson's concept of identity, I would characterize it as follows: it implies an indisoluble dialectic of individual and society, present and future, security and autonomy. It is this which gives it its existential character and which ensures that identity is not abstractly defined but is credibly postulated and can thus become an object of interdisciplinary dialogue where priority should be given to the search for future norms. But can such an aim serve as a key to the understanding of Christian symbols? Does this not involve turning to texts and traditions with questions which are removed from their original purpose, and thus distorting and falsifying their real meaning?

This approach would be totally unjustified were Christian teaching not primarily presented in symbolic form. 'All symbols provoke thought . . . they show in an exemplary way that there is more in myths and symbols than in our entire philosophy . . . Consider too the foundering of those systems of thought where symbols are imprisoned in an absolute knowledge'.[28] The German psychoanalyst Tilman Moser offered a highly emotional 'discount' in his recent work on religious socialization in which the following remarkable proposition occurs: Christian symbols 'subtly communicate all children's fears and longings, including those which are still unresearched'.[29] This implies that Christian symbols present a far greater richness than that tiny area of the human psyche, that up till now can be considered to be scientifically researched. Identity and human maturation are basically eschatological concepts that can never be defined empirically for they always precede human experience. Erikson's formulation of the various problem areas in respect of different age-levels can be related to the varying range of symbols within the Christian tradition. It is important to understand the problem areas within the context of the course of the human life-cycle, and only to construct them in their totality into a meaningful whole; for every development level leaves behind it ineradicable traces in the human psyche. The problem areas are:

1. The problem of the reciprocity of 'face-to-face recognition', paraphrased as the experience of the numinous.
2. The distinction between good and evil.
3. The dramatic shaping of activity.
4. The development of rules of conduct.
5. The experience of the solidarity of certainties.
6. The generative function of attention to that which will come.[30]

If we accept that a definite range of Christian symbols corresponds to the problems or areas of conflict outlined above, then it is possible to find a key that will jointly afford an understanding of both human beings and the Christian symbols themselves. For, as Hugo Rahner has shown, there is a point of departure common to both: in traditional terminology 'to bring about the birth of Christ in one's own soul'.[31] In contemporary terminology: 'to realize more completely an identity *coram Deo*'. To summarize:

1. Communication in the Church may be understood as a duel process of symbolic interaction: first, the official 'traditional' symbols can be brought to bear on the lives of individuals and of groups; second, communication takes the form of the resolution of individual conflict, usually through the 'privatization' of symbols.

2. Both processes of communication are ambiguous and in need of interpretation. Because the symbols of the Church are dogmatically

defined, and those that are private, psychologically defined, the two systems frequently operate in isolation from one another.

3. For religious psychology to be effective as pastoral psychology, it is essential to have a hermeneutical key which will unlock the symbolic interaction of both processes.

4. This can lie in the acceptance that in both symbolic systems—irrespective of the question of another and 'deeper' significance—we are concerned with the resolution on an inconceivable number of human problems.[32]

Finally, I should like to try to show how conflict corresponds to the various stages of the ontogenesis of ritualization, and to suggest some of the ways in which Christian symbols can be understood and interpreted as an aid to maturation.

CHRISTIAN SYMBOLS AS AN AID TO MATURATION

1. From the earliest beginnings of life, everyone retains a vague and unconscious memory of the indistinguishability of subject from object. In the present (usually to an extent corresponding to the emotional desire to be absorbed by the individuality of other people) this leads to a projection of a gigantic extended 'parent-image' from earliest childhood that provides a sensation of being part of them. Alternatively, it perpetuates the 'grandiose larger self' through the intake and absorption of the individuality of other people.[33] In a milder form, this conflict expresses itself in a deep longing for a mutual face-to-face recognition, accompanied by a numinous feeling of belonging. In view of this basic conflict, maturation would imply the insight (intellectually achieved and emotionally verified) that this kind of *unio mystico* is no longer possible but must be relinquished. All the formulae of blessing in the wealth of the Christian tradition point to the fundamental symbol of the personal oppositeness of God and man. This is most concisely expressed in the so-called 'blessing of Aaron' (Num 6: 24–26) to which Luther assigns a prime place in the Protestant service, and which is given a correspondingly important position in the Catholic liturgy. Similarly, Paul (1 Cor 13:12) expresses the eschatological ideal of human maturation and identity.

2. A small child 'learns' the difference between good and evil through the basic functions of his own body, which seeks to incorporate 'the good' and reject 'the bad'. It can appear only as a failure to handle this basic conflict and must be deemed a sign of immaturity, if the 'good' is confused with the 'pleasant', leading to a neurotic tendency towards oral incorporation (as is characteristic of our Western civilization), and if the 'bad' in one's self is no longer truly accepted,

but is rather projected onto others outside, and there, furiously and without awareness, opposed. But when, in antithesis to this, a symbolic meal occupies the central position in the Christian liturgy and a union with the *summum bonum* and the *communio sanctorum* is simultaneously promised, there is a symbolic reaffirmation of the critical objection to the absolutization of oral demands and aggressive exclusiveness. Against the background of a consumer society, the symbol of eating and drinking achieves today a new transparency and looks towards a maturation in the better differentiation of the spiritual.

3/4. The psychological blows of the play and school-age phases of development, consist dialectically in creative construction on the one hand, and the adoption of formal rules of conduct on the other. In this context immaturity can express itself as much in chaotic productivity as in dead formalism, in other words, in an absolute adherence to one or other polar extreme in the conflict. The Christian liturgy lives through a fruitful tension between Ordinary and Proper and affords the chance of both joyful recognition and unexpected encounter; the essential fact of these two things' relatedness to one another, is, according to Erikson, one of the fundamental preconditions of maturity and identity.

5. The lack of an established means of achieving a solidarity of convictions is undoubtedly reflected in the diffusion of, and crisis in, identity. The decisive question for the Church must therefore remain whether it is in a position in a given situation, to communicate reasonably its creed or 'symbols', so that young people can find their identity within them.

6. In the case of generativity, it is perhaps in the interests of clarity to leave an exposition of this ideal, formal and devoid of content, if it cannot be exemplified in concrete terms. The conflict which the notion of generativity involves, is actualized in the relationship between restriction and freedom, which has to be continually redefined during the transition from one generation to the next. If the old generation insists on too much restriction, it risks provoking the reaction of a revolutionary break with historical continuity. If it offers a freedom which borders on indifference, it will fail to harness the strength and vitality of the new generation for the construction of common fundamental values. Perhaps there is no more eloquent symbol than Christian baptism, which reveals, from a parental perspective, the essence of this problematic: Your child is not your property, but the property of God; it is, however, lent to you, entrusted to your responsibility and care.[34]

Perhaps the posing of such questions about the potential value of the symbols of the Church will at first succeed only in arousing hostility. This will certainly be the case if one considers that the established interpretation of Christian symbols (and here I am speaking of the pursuit of theology), has no other service to perform than to ensure the self-preservation of the Christian community. If, however, one extends the hope—and this is something I would passionately wish to do—that theology has an essential contribution to make to human survival and to the finding of identity among mankind in general, the possession of a common hermeneutical key, valid equally for theology and the humanities, seems to be a pressing necessity.

Translated by M. Chaytor

Notes

1. Sigmund Freud, *The Future of an Illusion* (1927).
2. Sigmund Freud, *A Childhood Memory of Leonardo da Vinci* (1910).
3. Sigmund Freud, *New Introductory Lectures on Psychoanalysis* (1933).
4. Ibid.
5. Ibid.
6. Ibid.
7. Cf. Joachim Scharfenberg, *Sigmund Freud und seine Religions—kritik als Herausforderung für den christlichen Glauben* (Göttingen, 1976).
8. Oskar Pfister, 'Neutestamentliche Seelsorge und psychoanalytische Therapie', *Imago* vol. 20 (1934), p. 431.
9. Oskar Pfister, 'Die Illusion einer Zukunft', *Imago* XIV (1928), pp. 149–84. Reprinted in: Nase & Scharfenberg, *Psychoanalyse und Religion* (Darmstadt, 1927), p. 132.
10. R. S. Lee, *Freud and Christianity* (London, 1967), p. 9.
11. Ibid., p. 80.
12. Ibid., p. 124.
13. R. S. Lee, *Psychology and Worship* (London, 1955), p. 14.
14. Ibid., pp. 16 & 19.
15. Ibid., p. 28.
16. Erik H. Erikson, 'Autobiographisches zur Identitätskrise', *Psyche* 27, no. 9 (1973), p. 811.
17. Ibid., p. 815.
18. Ibid., p. 811.
19. In *Psyche* 22 (1968), pp. 481–502.
20. Erik H. Erikson, *Toys and Reasons, Stages in the Ritualization of Experience* (New York, 1977).
21. Jürgen Habermas, *Erkenntnis und Interesse* (Frankfurt, 1968) (trans., *Knowledge and Human Interests*, London & Boston, 1971), p. 321.
22. Cf. Erikson, 'Autobiographishes', p. 816.

23. Ibid., p. 812.

24. Erik H. Erikson, *Einsicht und Verantwortung* (Stuttgart, 1966) (trans., *Insight and Responsibility,* London & New York, 1964), p. 205.

25. Ibid., p. 221.

26. Cf. Don S. Browning, *Generative Man* (Philadelphia, 1973).

27. Erik H. Erikson, *Identity and Life-cycle* (New York, 1965).

28. Paul Ricoeur, *L' Interpretation* (Paris, 1965).

29. Tilman Moser, *Gottesvergiftung* (Frankfurt, 1976), p. 82.

30. Erikson, *Toys and Reasons,* p. 114.

31. Cf. Hugo Rahner, *Symbole der Kirche* (Salzburg, 1964), pp. 29, 34, 43ff.

32. These ideas are developed in more detail in Joachim Scharfenberg, 'Kommunikation in der Kirche als symbolische Interaktion' in *Seelsorgeausbildung* (ed. W. Becher, Göttingen, 1976), pp. 43ff.

33. Cf. Heinz Kohut, *The Analysis of the Self* (New York, 1971).

34. In this context see also J. Scharfenberg, 'Psychoanalytische Randbemerkungen zum Problem der Taufe', *Theologische Quartalschrift* 154, no. 1 (1974), pp. 3ff.

PART II

*Rite and Passage in the Judaeo-Christian
Tradition: Some Examples*

Erich Zenger

Ritual and Criticism of Ritual in the Old Testament

THE cultic history of Old Testament Israel is one aspect of its history for which the sources are not exactly plentiful. In particular, the origins of most rites are shrouded in obscurity. This limitation also applies to the following attempt to demonstrate and evaluate the strong links between this cult and the collective and individual existence by means of some observations on the ancient tradition of cult in Israel.

BASIC TENETS OF OLD TESTAMENT ATTITUDES TO WORSHIP

Rites in Israel are characterized by an underlying tension. To a certain extent these rites stem from everyday situations in which Israel was one of many nations in the ancient world living under similar conditions. Hence concepts and exercises more or less comparable to those rites practised in Israel can be found in the countries surrounding it. In addition to this, belief in Yahweh possesses a specific and unmistakable overall structure and such a striking, 'substantial' core that it always tended to leave its mark on the rites it practised. The history of the rites practised in Israel is a continuous process of critical acceptance and productive re-interpretation of rites which Israel absorbed, shaped or altered from its encounters with other cultural 'worlds' and from its own social and anthropological 'world'. Belief in Yahweh proceeded in this respect along the same lines as in all other spheres in which it established itself. It collected, sifted and pronounced judgment in the name of Yahweh.

In order to grasp this continuous process of extending the influence of Yahweh to further aspects of life more precisely, we must first define the 'core' which functions in this respect as diacritical principle.[1] With the name Yahweh (= He reveals himself in experience) Israel designates 'from the start' that fundamental experience in which it experiences its existence, past, present and future, as a life bestowed by God in the eyes of whom it must freely be justified. The summary of this experience as expressed in the term *Yahwe* and encompassing the aspects 'He *has proven* himself with us and for us and proves himself continually' and 'He *wants* to prove Himself in and through us' provides the perspectival vanishing point towards which and from which all Israel's experiences, hope and challenge merge. At the same time this abbreviated formula makes apparent the fundamental incarnated dynamic of Yahweh's 'Yahweh-ness'. Yahweh does not exist without the world and mankind in whom he manifests himself as the power to freely give and desire to give life. And the same thing applies in reverse: Israel is 'the people of Yahweh' only when it makes it clear by its words and deeds that it knows about Yahweh. This is the root of the tension existing between Yahweh and his people and drawing them together; so that on the one hand these two poles possess their own (though different!) autonomy, while on the other hand being dependent on each other as regards their 'outlook on life', in that they are. In concrete terms this means that Israel can shape all spheres of its life as gifts from its God. At the same time it must do this so that the fundamental experience of 'life gratefully received which can thus be handed on', that is, 'a life both liberated and liberating in freedom' can be perceived as the perspective of all action demanded by theology and anthropology.

This view of Yahweh is also the yardstick by which to evaluate the cult forms and rites connected with belief in Yahweh which Israel acquired from other peoples and cultures or which evolved in Israel itself out of a variety of different situations. The fundamental tension caused by the polarity inherent in belief in Yahweh materializes itself in the polarity between rite and ethos, rite and faith, and service to humanity and service to God. This polarity structures the decalogue, for instance, in such a way that the fundamental experience is formulated in the title, which is consequently followed first by the 'theological cult commandments' and then by the 'anthropological-social commandments'. From this it becomes apparent that rite and ethos belong together and complement each other. This is also emphasized by the so-called portal liturgies (e.g., Ps 15) 'in which the pilgrim entering the sacred area is reminded to fulfil his duty to Yahweh in his daily life . . . The God of Israel is a god of righteousness. His cult is no primitive, magical injection of strength to the assembled community. Yahweh is the lord over all life. Whoever enters into his sacred presence is questioned about his daily behaviour. Divine service thus begins with the decisive question about obedience. The portal liturgies in particular indicate . . . how everything is connected. Whether included in or excluded from the specific cult sphere everything is subject to the power of God and its total demand, embracing all life'.[2] Rite and cult are thus only directed 'towards Yahweh' when they summarize, present in ritual form and give an impulse to what Yahweh desires for his people; namely brotherly, mutually liberating life. In this way social and anthropological aspects are fused.

Owing to the way it is bound into the overall context of life, the function of cult in Israel differs to a certain extent from the functions found in the surrounding countries.[3] These functions are mostly based on the idea that cult and the various ritual actions symbolize the activation or liberation of secret powers by means of which gods and men respectively are assured their living strength. Cult and rite can be seen as a striving for assurance for two reasons; the intention is either to strengthen a godhead that is too weak, or to protect men from mysterious divine and demonic powers which threaten them. Cult and rite of this kind do not liberate men or give them the confidence to develop themselves and to freely mould their world; on the contrary, they represent the culmination of the fundamental alienation of men. This is precisely where belief in Yahweh differs, owing to its particular image of God and man. The rites permitted and developed are intended to symbolize and perfect that creative freedom implied by his very name, Yahweh.

RITUAL FORMATION OF TURNING POINTS IN THE AGRICULTURAL YEAR

The close connection between rites in Israel and the life of the individual Israelite can be seen from the three main annual festivals: the Mazzen feast or the Feast of Unleavened Bread, harvest or the Feast of Weeks and the Feast of Tabernacles.[4] The rites celebrated on these feast-days indicate an anthropological and social context—from both the religio-historical and the religio-phenomenological point of view—which is not inherently because of Yahweh but in a large measure corresponds to the (Canaanite) agrarian structure. The three feasts articulate and embrace the course of the peasant's year and their rites symbolize what people who believe their daily lives to be dependent on the gods experience in that they regard the fertility of nature manifested in the harvest as the culmination of the gods. The Feast of Unleavened Bread celebrated the beginning of harvest; for the first seven days of the harvest only a bread made of new corn was eaten, prepared without leaven (symbolizing the new beginning). The completion of the harvest was symbolized by the sacrificial rite of the Feast of Weeks when two loaves of bread baked from flour ground out of the new corn (with leaven) were brought to the shrine. The Feast of Tabernacles was celebrated in autumn when the fruit, olives and grapes were gathered. By means of dancing and festivities in the huts put up in the vineyards, orchards and olive groves for the harvest, socially integrating aspects (community at work and at play) and Dionysiac cult aspects (drinking the new season's wine from the wine-press, selection of brides) were fused in ritual form.

In its encounter with Canaanite agrarian culture, the religion of Yahweh did not simply abolish or forbid these feasts and their rites. On the contrary, it received them critically and infused them to a certain extent with new meaning, thus provided the anthropological and social basis for interpreting the rites as "signs of Yahweh". This critical approach is manifested in several different ways, described variously as to adapt to Yahweh, to historicize, to mythicize and to treat anthropologically.

In Israel, through their connection with Yahweh, these rites assume a new directness. They are symbols of gratitude, praise and the hopeful expression of trust in Yahweh. They are a fulfilment 'for Yahweh' by which man opens himself to receive his life as a gift from his God. Israel comes face to face with its God by means of these rites; not merely to assure itself of its God but rather to acknowledge his divinity and goodness. This doxological focussing on Yahweh means that both cult and rites are freed from the necessity of being a means of salvation for God, man and the world.

This link with Yahweh also means that these feasts are drawn into a historical context, in the sense that the rites are performed in reminiscence of historical occasions on which Yahweh proved himself to Israel. The Feast of Unleavened Bread becomes a feast of the exodus, the unleavened, quickly baked loaves symbolizing the haste and unexpectedness with which Yahweh freed his people from slavery in Egypt. The novelty of the unleavened bread reminds Israel that in commemorating the exodus the feast of unleavened bread it is encountering the God who during and since the exodus has taken the part of Israel by means of his eternal grace. The harvest festival was probably historicized only in the period after the exile, when it was celebrated to commemorate the gift of the Torah in the Sinai. In the same way that the fertility of nature and the harvest were demonstrated by the offering of the loaves as the gift of the God of exodus, the guiding, life-giving word of the Torah was given by Yahweh to his people at the exodus as the burgeoning seed that would in time yield the harvest.[5] The historical attachment of the Feast of the Tabernacles seems to have been a very complex process. According to Lev 23, 42f., the seven days spent living in huts made of branches are intended to remind the Israelites of the exodus, wandering through the wilderness, when Yahweh caused his people 'to live in tents'. This reference to the permanent state of being en route in the wilderness is somewhat anachronistic in that the 'tabernacles' of this semi-nomadic people wandering through the desert were certainly tents made of cloth or skins and not 'huts made of foliage'. Rabbinical tradition thus made these tabernacles into symbols of the security Yahweh gave his people by his light (*kabod*) which enfolded them like tents during their journey. But it is also possible that the generally happy character of the feast played a part in this, if the feast symbolizes Israel as a large community living in tents and led by Yahweh. From about the period of the exile two elements of the autumn festival were instituted as feast days in their own right, and preceding the main feast in time. New Year's Day thus assumed more of an emphasis on the theological aspects of creation, whereas[6] the Day of Atonement was to cover the purification of the temple and the expiation of the community.[7] The linking of the feasts to historical events removed them from too close a connection with natural processes, which in the ancient world were frequently invested with divine or magical powers. This division was then further emphasized by the fact that the feasts were no longer celebrated after the conclusion of the harvest in any one year, but on specific dates established on the calendar.[8]

Narrowly linked to the historicization of the old agrarian feast days is the growing emphasis on their function as a force for social integration. Since in Israel the rites connected with these feasts are not to be seen either as 'imitations' of mythically predetermined natural processes nor as compulsory duties to the godhead (Yahweh), they are able to develop the form of a genuinely human and humane fulfilment. The deuteronomical movement in particular stresses this in that it repeatedly calls attention to joy and play as essential factors of these feasts which it sees as transmitting joyful and liberating experiences. In addition, the effect the feasts have on drawing the community closer together is promoted not merely by transferring its ritual focal points to Jerusalem; [9] the social aspect is also intensified by the practice of dropping all social differences and barriers during the communally celebrated feast day. Hence the rites are not just actions performed by the individual, but are integrated into the whole 'people of Yahweh'.

This process of historicization and 'adaptation to conditions in Israel', as outlined above, could thus be described in the last analysis as a specific way in which the old rites were gradually mythicized and consequently changed.[10] It was not a case of selecting historical events at random, but rather events from ancient history connected with the foundation of Israel (Exodus and Sinai). These basic experiences were commemorated in the feasts as fundamental stories whose effectiveness consisted in a combination of rite and quasi-mythical language. In its cult myths Israel returned to the origins of its salvation history and attempted a *restitutio ad integrum* which was clearly hoped for as a freely granted gift of Yahweh, thus making apparent the breaking of the myth. This partial fusion of cult and myth is 'not primarily a question of absorbing alien myths; instead, it should be seen as a kind of mythically orientated attitude towards the content of their own traditions'.[11] By mythicizing its cults, Israel is to a certain extent linking them to Yahweh.

Prophetic criticism of the feasts and rites of Israel is really concerned with all these aspects of re-interpreting Israel's existing rites.[12] The prophets protest that the rites do not lead to an encounter with Yahweh, but that they are mainly an adulation of nature and its fertility (cf. the cult polemics in Hosea) and a celebration for its own sake (cf. Am 4:4f.; 5:21; Jes 22:13). Above all, these feasts lack the socially constructive power which should be inherent in them as feasts of Yahweh, and as rites performed by men who by means of these rites should be able to experience their collective life history as the co-existence of liberated individuals with equal rights. The asperity of the prophets' criticism of rites is not aimed at the rites as such. Their intention is rather to demonstrate openly that Israel is not in a state worthy or even capable of rites unless Yahweh's approach to salvation and justice is realized as the basic principle of co-existence. Hence prophetic criticism of rites combines social criticism and dogmatic criticism: a rite is only pleasing to Yahweh when it promotes human co-existence. And the same applies in reverse: a rite which has the effect of developing and liberating human life must at the same time open this life up to experiencing human life as a gift of Yahweh, and it is as such that it must be accounted for.

RITUAL MASTERY AND MOTIVATION OF BASIC HUMAN SITUATIONS

The question of the 'effectiveness' of rites presents itself above all in those basic situations in which the ambivalence of human life is particularly acute and which require to be mastered and filled with meaning. These are birth, marriage and death. Here too the religion of Yahweh demonstrates its critical, integrating strength in that it is extremely hesitant in giving religious connotations to the rites associated with these events in the ancient world.

In Israel conception and birth are especially connected to two kinds of rites, namely the purification rites of the parents and the circumcision of male offspring. As with many other peoples of the ancient world, the Israelites regarded sexual processes such as ejaculation, menstruation and post-natal discharge as consequences of cult impurity: that is, those marked by any of these 'blemishes' were excluded from cult practices and were only admitted again if they observed the prescribed ritual actions and given periods of time. This condemnation of the processes connected with conception and birth as ritually impure stems from the fact that they were interpreted as a limitation of the creative life-force of the man and of the mother who lost blood when giving birth.[13] Blood was considered to be the source of all life; hence the mother, through this loss of blood entered into the sphere of death, and had to be cut off from the ritual life of the community and above all from Yahweh, the God of life, until she qualified as being 'alive' once more. After the period of purification, and after the washing and offerings of the purification ritual she is officially received into the community again by the priest. Although it must be emphasized that such rites are firmly rooted in an out-moded world view, one should nevertheless consider that these rites had a liberating and supportive function in the crucial situations of life. The doctrine of Yahweh also possessed two features which served to ward off the magical dimension that can so easily become linked with purification rites of this kind. Firstly, it excluded any polytheistic or demonic model by means of which the impurity was caused by some 'opponent' of Yahweh. Hence the ritual purification could not be interpreted as a ritual protecting the individual in the face of or even against Yahweh. On the contrary, it became a 'gateway to life' made possible by Yahweh himself. Secondly, the purification rites, e.g., of a woman after childbirth, had a graduated theological significance. Whereas the prescribed period of social isolation and the washing should be regarded as a deep-rooted tradition, the purification culminates in an offering of expiation and in a burnt-sacrifice offered by the priest to the godhead as an act of thanksgiving and homage on the part of the mother (or the parents?).[14] By means of this act of homage to Yahweh, the God of life, at least some of the links with worldly aspects were removed, thus revealing the deeper theological tendency which a genuine Yahweh rite had to have in the context of birth; namely, the acknowledgment of Yahweh as the giver of all life.

Another ritual practised in Israel in context with birth is circumcision.[15] The origin and original meaning of this universally practised Semitic ritual are obscure. In the first instance such ceremonies were mostly understood as initiation rituals or 'rites of passage' by means of which the sexually-mature youth was received into the society of men, the ritual itself symbolizing a sign of race or purification rite. Or one might emphasize more strongly the objective connection between the ritual, fertility and marriage, regarding the ritual as 'the act of consecration of the young man through which the fertility of marriage should be guaranteed . . . A decisive factor in this context is the analogous denotations and customs connected with the first use of the fruit tree: the trees should remain for three years without pruning or picking the fruit; in the fourth year the fruit should be brought to Yahweh as an offering of thanksgiving, as it were, the circumcision; and in the fifth year the tree should begin to be used (Lev 19:23f.). In the same way that the fertility of nature must be bought from its divine owner, the man about to celebrate his marriage must beforehand make an offering to the Lord about human fertility, in the form of circumcision with its accompanying atonement through blood'.[16] In Israel this ritual was received as a 'birth ritual', the process of its theological interpretation being similar to the reception of the Canaanite agrarian feasts outlined above. The puzzling text Ex 4:24–6 attempts on the one hand to justify the transfer of circumcision to infancy by means of an event connected with Moses while on the other hand interpreting circumcision as a 'sign of the exodus'. Circumcision is a ritual through which Israel commemorates its acceptance as a son by Yahweh (cf. Ex 4:22) who permits the circumcised to share in the history of salvation which Yahweh had begun for his collective son, Israel, in the exodus. The theological and 'sacramental' nature of circumcision becomes much clearer from the time of the exile onwards. In hierarchical theology circumcision is regarded as a ratification and symbol of that special covenant which Yahweh made with Abraham (Gen 17). In the same way that the sabbath was hallowed, circumcision was made into a decisive sign of faith symbolizing and documenting adherence to Judaism. Anyone who wished to be converted to the Jewish religious community had to be circumcised (cf. Jdt 14:10; Esther 8:17 LXX); conversely, the Jewish apostates at the time of the Maccabeans even tried to 'remove the marks of circumcision' (cf. 1 Maccabees 1:15).

The rite of circumcision thus had the function of incorporating birth as an anthropologically and socially important event into the sphere of the religiously conceived national history. Precisely this religious aspect of circumcision is stressed by theological ritual criticism, above all as formulated in Deuteronomy and in the Book of Jeremiah. In essence, circumcision must be a circumcision of the heart; if this is not so, circumcision signifies nothing (cf. Deut 10:16: Jer 4:4). Circumcision symbolizes the offering of the entire being to Yahweh and can therefore meaningfully be performed at the beginning of life.[17]

Marriage in Israel remained singularly free of ritual. The ceremony of marriage was regarded primarily as a legal procedure (the main emphasis was on the regulation of property), while the marriage celebrations were defined more in terms of tradition than ritual. This is all the more surprising in that in the ancient world of the Orient sexuality and fertility were in large measure determined by nature myths. Marriage was therefore a more or less explicit ritual representation of the original mythical marriage; it was not regarded so much as an anthropological or social situation, but rather as an event whose 'rules' (time, place, dress, of marital sex) were drawn from the fertility of divinized nature.[18] Hence the profanity of the marriage ceremony in Israel is presumably to be seen as a religious polemic distinguising it from other oriental countries. However one cannot overlook the fact that this resulted in a ritual deficit which the people then filled with a series of pseudo-ritual procedures, above all the well-founded Old Testament polemic against every possible form of sexual or fertility rites.[19] The fear of demonic powers whose powers were believed to dominate both marriage and birth (cf. Tob 3:7ff.) also led to a variety of magical practices,[20] which could have been avoided if the marriage ceremony had been more directly linked to faith in Yahweh by means of a more explicit ritual connection, with rites based on a firmer anthropological foundation.

The religion of Yahweh manifests equally ambivalent rites in connection with death as it does with birth and marriage. In the first place it reacted somewhat polemically towards the marriage and funeral rites practised in the region, which combined fundamental human events and the cult rites prescribed by the Canaanite religion. The ritual of the dead begins with a ritual of lamentation symbolizing solidarity with the dead person and the loss experienced by the group at his death; there then follows a burial ritual intended to ensure the 'new' existence of the dead. In the old tradition of the Orient this was closely linked to the mythical concept of the god who dies and is reborn. This is precisely why the religion of Yahweh for a long time avoided any connection between this ritual and the official cult of Yahweh, because Yahweh is a god of the living and not of the dead. These anthropological and socially highly meaningful rites were thus reduced to the level of a profane tradition connected with death. Whoever performed them, or had to perform them, became impure and had to expiate this impurity by means of complex purification rites. This rejection of traditional burial rites is further intensified by the fact that the priest, as cult representative, is forbidden to take part at all (cf. Lev 21:1.11). The intention of this 'de-ritualization' is evidently that a clear demarcation line should be drawn round the sphere of death, which is not yet integrated theologically. But here too we see the sharp polemic directed, for example, against magical practices such as the sacrifice of hair or blood to the dead (cf. Lev 19:27f.) and the interrogation of the dead (cf. Lev 19:31), in order that this ritual omission should not be fully comprehended or taken for granted by the people. However, in the period after the exile there was a partial re-evaluation of these rites. The problem of death was then overcome theologically by the confession of faith in Yahweh who precisely in the matter of death proves himself to be the life-giving God of salvation (cf. Ps 49:73). Together with the greater emphasis on mutual solidarity which manifested itself in mourning and funerary rituals,[21] it then became more possible to give ritual form to the critical situation of death.

CONCLUSIONS

1. Rites in Israel have extraordinarily strong links with significant turning-points in both the individual and the collective existence; and many features of the rituals originate in other countries in the Middle East.

2. The rites which are intended to imbue the turning points of life with significance have a particularly strong therapeutic and liberating effect to the extent that they should help to overcome threatening situations by means of ritual.

3. All rites share (though to a differing degree) a tendency towards social integration, in that the rite is seen as the impulse to regard oneself as participating in a common ritual as a member of the community, and also because prophetic criticism calls for the socially critical implications of the rites as the rites of a community living by the demands of Yahweh.

4. To some extent all the rites demonstrate a kerygmatic tendency in that their ritual ambivalence is rendered so precise by means of this unequivocal reference to Yahweh, the giver, guarantor challenger of all life, that the rite finally becomes an encounter with the God of salvation.

Translated by Sarah Twohig

Notes

1. Cf. in greater detail P. Weimar and E. Zenger, *Exodus Geschichten und Geschichte der Befreiung Israels* (Stuttgart, 1975); E. Zenger, 'Die Mitte der alttestamentlichen Glaubensgeschichte' in *Katechetische Blätter,* 101 (1976), pp. 3–16.

2. H. J. Kraus, *Gottesdienst im alten und im neuen Bund in Biblisch-theologische Aufsätze* (Neukirchen-Vluyn, 1972), p. 198.

3. Cf. F. Stolz, *Das Alte Testament* (Gütersloh, 1974), pp. 94–115; W. H. Schmidt, *Alttestamentlicher Glaube in seinter Geschichte* (Neukirchen-Vluyn,[2] 1975), pp. 113–29.

4. The problem of the secondary connexion between the Feast of Unleavened Bread and the Passover cannot be dealt with here any more than the question as to the origin of the Feast of the Passover.

5. With regard to the historicization of the Feast of Weeks cf. 2 Chr 15:10 and the Book of Jubilees. 'Perhaps the priests were already aware of this historical derivation when they caused the revelation of Sinai to take place in "the third month", i.e., in the period of the Feast of Weeks, unless the subsequent nature of the feast was based on Ex 19:1' (W. H. Schmidt, op. cit., p. 121).

6. Cf. D. J. A. Clines, 'The Evidence for an Autumnal New Year in Pre-Exilic Israel Reconsidered', in *Journal of Biblical Literature* 93 (1974), pp. 22–40.

7. Cf. R. de Vaux, *Das Alte Testament und seine Lebensordnungen,* II (Freiburg, 1960), ch. 18, section 1.

8. After the transfer of the New Year to spring, the seven-day long Feast of Unleavened Bread was fixed on the fourteenth to the twenty-first day of the first month: i.e., the subsequent Nisan.

9. Cf. the programme of this 'cult centralization' in Ex 34:23.

10. From the point of view of religious history, this was almost a re-mythicization of the previously de-mythicized Canaanite feasts.

11. W. Pannenberg, 'Späthorizonte des Mythos in biblischer und christlicher Uberlieferung', in *Poetik und Hermeneutik,* IV (Munich, 1971), p. 502.

12. Cf. H. Schüngel-Straumann, *Gottesbild und Kultkritik vorexilischer Propheter* (Stuttgard 1972).

13. Cf. W. Kornfeld, *Das Buch Leviticus* (Düsseldorf, 1972), pp. 72–103.

14. On the history of sacrificial classification, cf. R. Rendtorff, *Studien zur Geschichte des Opfers im Alten Israel* (Neukirchen-Vluyn, 1967), pp. 19f.

15. Cf. W. Zimmerli, *Grundriss der alttestamentlichen Theologie* (Stuttgart, 1972), pp. 114f.

16. W. Eichrodt, *Theologie des Alten Testaments,* I (seventh ed., Stuttgart, 1972), 4, note 185.

17. On the spiritualization of cult in general, cf. H. J. Hermission, *Sprache und Ritus im altisraelitischen Kult* (Neukirchen-Vluyn, 1965).

18. Cf. for example the Ugaritic myths 'The Birth of Sahr and Salim' and 'The Marriage of Jarih and Nikkal'; summarized in H. Gese & K. Rudolph, *Die Religionen Altsyriens, Altarabiens und der Mandäer* (Stuttgart, 1970), pp. 80–84.

19. Cf. Hos 4:12–14; Is 17:9–11; Jer 2:20; 3, 2; Is 56:9–57, 13.

20. Cf. the many amulets with sexual symbols found by archeologists in ancient cities in Israel.

21. The Book of Tobit, for example, categorizes the burial ritual as a 'work of mercy'.

Anthonius Scheer

Is the Easter Vigil a Rite of Passage?

SINCE Odo Casel published his famous study on the nature and meaning of the oldest Christian celebration of Easter,[1] the attention of many historians and liturgists has been drawn to this primary and most important of all feasts. During the last decades it has been subjected to various attempts at renewal (Pius XII, Vatican II).[2] Among other topics this research has been concerned with the somewhat obscure origin of our Easter celebration. This delving into the past is important because it may give our search for a renewed paschal liturgy an indispensable orientation.

After going through these studies, I nevertheless had the impression that up till now they have been so dominated by the historical aspect that the consideration of the nature of the paschal celebration has only received incomplete and indirect treatment. In this article I want to take a step in the direction of the question: what is the relation between the celebration of Easter as a cultic phenomenon and what today has come to be called a 'rite of passage', after Arnold van Gennep?[3]

This question was prompted by, among other things, the classical terminology used for the celebration of Easter, and which Christien Mohrmann took as the title of one of her essays: 'Pascha—passio—transitus'.[4] At first sight, indeed, the terms 'transitus' and 'passage' seem to be closely related.

I start with a survey of the historical research insofar as it is connected with our question; this is followed by an attempt at a liturgical-theological interpretation from this angle, and I conclude with some observations which may be of use to contemporary liturgical practice.

THE ORIGIN OF THE EASTER CELEBRATION

The time covered by the investigation can be conveniently marked off. I shall not go beyond the period when the particular facets of the Easter celebration began to spread outwards: namely, the fourth century. It was then that Good Friday, Easter Sunday, Ascension and Whitsunday appeared in the calendar as separate celebrations with a more distinct theme: Good Friday became the day of the Lord's suffering and death, while Sunday concentrated on his resurrection.[5] We cannot go back further than the second half of the second century because only then do we meet with the first evidence of a Christian Easter celebration. The two centuries between these two points in time provide us with the data required for our investigation.

1. The date when Easter should be celebrated was considered as very important by the early Christians.[6] But there was no agreement on this in the second century. Some communities, particularly in Asia Minor, thought that Easter had to be celebrated on a fixed date, the 14th or 15th nisan, which the Jews also observed, in spite of the fact that it could be celebrated on any day of the week.[7] This tradition agrees with the gospel of St John which dates the death of Jesus on the day the lambs were slaughtered in the temple, and also with certain passages in St Paul. Other communities thought that Easter should be celebrated in the night of the Sunday following on the Jewish date. This tradition stems from the synoptic gospels where the Lord's supper coincides with the Jewish celebration of the Pasch and the resurrection takes place on the first day of the week. In this controversy Rome supported the second view.

This matter of the Easter date has nothing to do with anti-Judaism but rather reflects a contrast within the communities of the Church between various evangelical traditions [8] where the opposition between the original Jewish-Christian and pagan-Christian spiritualities may well have played a secondary rôle.[9]

2. It was also necessary to fix the date in order to establish the period of Lent which preceded the Easter celebration.[10]

3. Because of the problem about the date and the position taken up by the Roman community, Sunday observance won the day and this was definitively confirmed by the Council of Nicea (325). Up till now the available data fail to show which of the two paschal regulations is the older or how far they reach back into the apostolic age, which rules out any historical preference so far.[11] The rejection of the quartodeciman position should not be understood as a matter of orthodoxy but as one of inter-community discipline.

4. The original Christian celebration of Easter took place from the evening until dawn. In all probability it consisted of readings, preach-

ing and the eucharist. Tradition has preserved a few second-century homilies, particularly those attributed to Melito and the pseudo-Hippolyte.[12] It was a night of vigil for the Lord. Having said this, we have put together the outer aspects of the oldest Easter celebration as far as we know it. In addition, Kretschmar stresses the fact that the form of the second century Easter celebration would remain akin to the kind of family liturgy, inherited from the days of the apostles, where the homily of the leader would fulfil an important function.[13]

Insofar as the theme of the celebration is concerned an important development occurred around the end of the second century.[14] The quartodeciman communities of Asia Minor appear to approach the Lord's mystery mainly on the typological basis of the sacrifice of the paschal lamb according to the narrative of Exodus 12. In this they followed the line indicated by Paul and John who pointed to the Lord in his passover as the new lamb, replacing the old one whose blood saved Israel from destruction. However, particularly the Alexandrines, Clement and Origen, saw the key in another typology: namely, the passage of the old Israel through the water towards the liberation from Egyptian slavery according to Exodus 14. They applied this to the Christian community as it celebrated Easter: we, too, celebrate our delivery from death leading to a new life in virtue of, and thanks to, the Lord's passage in his passover, through death to resurrection. The data lead us to conclude that the lamb typology was practically universal during the second and third centuries and that gradually the Alexandrine exodus typology took over in the West by way of the writings of St Ambrose.[15] This is why it is sometimes said that the lamb typology was probably the original one among Christians [16]: Easter is the commemoration of the Lamb Jesus Christ sacrificed in death for the delivery of his new people.

6. This supposition is reinforced by the fact that the exodus typology of the Alexandrines was inspired by Philo's idea of Easter. The Old Testament term 'pascha' of Exodus 12 which can be translated into Greek as 'metabasis'—Yahweh's passing over us to protect the first-born [17]—was translated by Philo as 'diabasis'—to pass through something, as the old Israel passed through the waters from slavery to delivery, from death to life. Philo saw the Pasch as a 'passage' from a ruinous situation to one of salvation. And so, for Origen, too, Easter is primarily the celebration of the passage through death towards the true life in the footsteps of the Lord. 'Diabasis' is rendered in Latin as 'transitus', a word which passed into the Vulgate through Jerome.

Over against this *transitus* concept, however, there is another one which links the term 'pascha', through etymologically inaccurately, with the Greek 'pathos' and the Latin 'passio'. Then Easter is seen as the celebration of the '*passio*' of Jesus Christ, an expression which not only implies suffering and death but that this event is a victory. Easter is the celebration of the victorious passion and death of the Lord, and this victory is manifested in his resurrection. This *passio*-concept, widespread in East and West, had a great influence until the days of Augustine who repeatedly insisted on the *transitus*-concept as the true one.[18]

In other words, the original Church shows that there was an evolution in the concept of Easter, from the *passio-pascha* to the *transitus-pascha,* corresponding to the typologies of the lamb and the passage through the Red Sea respectively. But this evolution seems to result in a prevalence of the *transitus*-idea only in the fourth century.

7. One may well wonder why this evolution went on so quietly compared with that about the date of Easter. The reason is that in spite of a difference of emphasis the basic idea of the Christian Easter was not really affected by the evolution. In both concepts Easter is the celebration of Jesus' saving deed in its totality, from the incarnation to his being placed at the right hand of the Father, with its climax in the event of the cross.

The supporters of the *transitus*-concept take too little account of the Lord's passion; those that support the *passio*-concept do the same with regard to his resurrection and ascension. Moreover, both the Old Testament types of the blood of the lamb and the passage through the Red Sea envisage the bringing of life and salvation. In spite of the differences in emphasis, both approaches allowed one to celebrate the same total and universal saving event of Christ and his people.

8. Nevertheless, in the end the *transitus*-concept won the day. How can we explain this? [19] First of all, one may refer to the fact that the acceptance of the *transitus*-concept in the course of the fourth century developed simultaneously with the deploying of the liturgical celebrations of the mystery of Christ on Good Friday, Easter Sunday, the fortieth day and the fiftieth day. In other words, the *transitus-pascha* seems to coincide with a mentality which attempted to put the various aspects of the one paschal mystery side by side in some kind of historical order. Moreover, the breakthrough of the *transitus*-idea seems to have taken place in a period which was less sensitive than before to the original theology of the cross and which was rather characterized by a kind of theological Docetism which paid less attention to the Lord as human and suffering than to his glorious and divine life in heaven. Finally, the *transitus*-idea seems to have prevailed in a period when the saving influence of the Lord on the believer was particularly characterized as deifying man on the ground of his incarnation [20]: he became man in order that man should be deified, so that the emphasis passes

from the passion to the incarnation and the incarnation is directly related to our life as renewed by the resurrection. In the fourth century
there are already Christian authors who see the Lord's passion as the
preparation for his resurrection. This approach will lead to a way of
celebrating Easter where Good Friday is not simply experienced as a
transitory phase but where Christ's resurrection is at the same time
seen as the real point of the celebration. By then, the unity of the
paschal spirituality and the paschal liturgy, which was characteristic of
the earliest Church, fell apart, once and for all. I would like to make
two observations with regard to all this. In the first place, I have not
said that this development was caused by the *transitus-pascha;* but I
have drawn attention to the fact that the definitive acclimatization of
this view took place in East and West in the prevailing theological and
spiritual climate of that time. Secondly, I wish to draw attention to the
differentiated character of this development, for example, Augustine,
while supporting the *transitus*-concept, also upheld the original paschal
spirituality which was distinguished by the way in which it embraced
the totality of the event.[21]

9. Is there still something else that should be mentioned about the
shape of the Easter celebration in the third and the beginning of the
fourth century, apart from what has been said under no. 4? Tertullian
and Hippolyte are the first to link the performing of the initiation
explicitly with the celebration of Easter, although the quartodeciman
homilies of the second century already contained allusions to baptism
as well as to the eucharist.[22] All the same, one should not conclude
from this that Easter Day was for them already exclusively the same as
initiation day. On the contrary, there was a general conviction that
baptism could take place at any time. Nor can one conclude from the
remarks made by Tertullian and Hippolyte that the initiation took place
during the Easter celebration: their remarks are far too general for that.
Still less can one try to prove that initiation took place in the context
and presence of the community: this practice was unknown in the early
Church. The first evidence of initiation being a part of the Easter celebration stems from the homilies of Asterius Sophistes, in the first half
of the fourth century and allows the conclusion that round about the
end of the third century initiation took place locally during the Easter
vigil.[23] These homilies show, however, that account was taken of the
baptism of children. For the rest, the various communities had their
own customs during the fourth century, as, for instance, in Alexandria,
where baptism took place in the context of the Good Friday rites in
378. One also notices a certain reserve in the writings of Ambrose and
Augustine who, indeed, link their *transitus*-interpretation of Easter
explicitly with initiation when talking to the catechumens but not when

talking to the faithful about Scripture and worship.[24] In so far as the question of initiation being a part of the Easter celebration is concerned one may conclude that the spreading of the *transitus* view made the administration of baptism during the vigil and the Easter celebration at least possible, so that in the long run it got a permanent place in the pattern of the vigil celebration.

10. The fourth-century data show that locally, in any case, the song of praise on Easter night was part of the Easter celebration. This liturgical phenomenon stems from the earliest Easter homilies, and found its hymnic shape in the fourth century and its final form in, e.g., the *exultet* hymns of the western liturgy.[25] Although this element has no immediate connection with our question, it is typical of this liturgical celebration and the theme of light and darkness in this hymn sung during the night provided an obvious and cosmically rooted opportunity to elaborate and express the idea of the *transitus-pascha*.

AN ATTEMPT AT INTERPRETATION

The question is: what exactly is the nature of the originally Christian celebration of Easter? Is it a commemoration rite meant to recall the bygone Pasch of the Lord to the mind of the believer, or is it a celebration of a mystery which aims at actualizing the saving event of Jesus' Pasch in the present in order to bring about salvation? Is it a rite primarily performed in view of enabling the faithful to participate in what the original event brought about, or is it a celebration aimed at making the believing community itself go through this original event in a ritual way?

The answer to the first question seems to be provided only too clearly by Christian antiquity. Augustine very explicitly rejected the purely commemorative interpretation of the Easter celebration.[26] But more important for our argument is that to typify the Easter celebration as a commemorative rite does not fit in with the historical fact that the community itself experienced this night as a particular moment in time, which is why it could sing about 'this night' because of its outstanding nature. This ritual phenomenon, unique in Christian worship, is a vital point that must be explained. It shows that this night has its own value with regard to the situation in which the community is saved: people celebrate a night of redemption for which there is no replacement in the actual existence of the faithful. Moreover, the original community did not itself invent this song of praise about the night of Easter. It is said that this interpretation is clearly related to the Jewish family celebration of the Pasch which contained among other things the delivery of the paschal haggada.[27] To the question why this particular night was singled out by the community as the moment of salvation *par excellence,* the answer is that this is the night when the Lord brought about salvation, the night of his Pasch.

This night does not derive its special character from its unique place in the time cycle—equinox, full moon, beginning of the year—but from the fact that it is the night of the Lord's death and resurrection, and all the cosmic accidents are the obvious elements with which to situate this event in time and to actualize it. With this in mind, we can also understand why the early Christians quarrelled over the determination of the right time for the celebration. It was not the fact that the Easter celebration should take place in the night because this was traditional and a matter of course, proper to the celebration of Easter as such, and therefore is common with the Jews. It was rather about the fact that this night and no other must be understood as the night of Jesus' death and resurrection. The questions about the dating of the night of Easter arose from the conviction that Jesus' Pasch contains for us the supreme value of reality and consequently can and must be anchored in the order of time. From these thoughts about the Christian paschal haggada and the dating of Easter it follows that this night is seen as the moment of salvation, because it is the night of the passing of the Lord, dead and risen. For the original community this night constituted a marking point in time insofar as at that point the mourning period of Lent drew to a close and passed over into the festal period of the *pentecosté* through the celebration of the eucharist.

We do not do justice to Easter if we take it simply as a commemorative rite. The community experiences this night as charged with salvation because it is the night of the Lord's saving deed, or better: the deed of the dead and risen Lord. When one tries to let this conviction get hold of one, it seems bizarre that at some point the unity of the paschal celebration was allowed to disperse itself into a number of partial celebrations with the idea of arranging them in some historical order. Could this have anything to do with a changing view of the Easter celebration? If so, where do we look for the beginnings of this change?

I find it difficult to escape the impression that it has something to do with the problematic issue of *pascha-passio* and *pascha-transitus*, although the original community probably did not distinguish between the two. The two approaches show some points where the divergence is quite clear. The *pascha-passio* tradition points more explicitly and directly to the suffering Lord who, precisely in and through his suffering, reaches resurrection. It is precisely death which contains the germ of life. According to John's presentation of the passion, it is precisely on the cross that victory is manifested. It is precisely the Lord's self-sacrifice as the new lamb which inaugurates liberation and the new life. The key to this lies precisely in his death which appears to be a sleep. The *pascha-passio* tradition hides a powerful and profound spirituality of the cross which summarizes the whole of the Lord's saving activity in his *passio*, a favourite idea of St Paul. The community celebrates this event of the cross in this night, convinced that it is concerned in it and that it is charged with achieving this in itself. And so Easter is the celebration of the new paschal lamb, Jesus Christ. Not for nothing does this tradition operate in terms of the typology of the old paschal lamb, particularly its blood which meant protection when Yahweh passed by the Israelite dwellings in the case of the first-born of the Egyptian families. It is the blood of the new paschal lamb which safeguards us from ruin and death. The mystique of the *pascha-passio* seems to be essentially a Christ-centred mystique, and the corresponding paschal celebration above all a celebration of Christ.

In my view, the *pascha-transitus* tradition shows another emphasis, perhaps inspired by the catechetical and moralizing trend of the Alexandrines. *Diabasis* or *transitus* signifies an evolving movement from a starting-point to a terminus: from evil to good, from darkness to light, from death to life. Here the passing is central, and consequently the enabling of this passage. This view presupposes two poles, and man is understood to have to move from one to the other, and not the other way round. Whereas the *pascha-passio* tradition understood the resurrection as inherent in the death of Jesus, the *pascha-transitus* tradition understands the resurrection as the anti-pole of death, and one has to achieve this *transitus* in order to truly share in the saving mystery of the Lord. The Easter celebration is then the sharing in the *transitus* of the Lord, and the important point is that one reaches indeed the other side, like the Lord. This *transitus* mystique also finds a corresponding typology in the *pascha* of the old people: the passage of the people through the water protected by Yahweh from the land of slavery to the land of freedom and promise.

From this angle, I am struck by the following points. First, this mystical approach is more explicitly and directly concerned with the followers of the Lord: we are the new people who, like the Lord, must go through this passage in order to reach life and light. Secondly, the *transitus*-idea is here essential and links up with the Alexandrine anagogical interpretation of Scripture and worship.[28] Thirdly, the terminus—the resurrection—entails an independence with regard to the starting-point—suffering and death—, and both poles are in mutual contrast. We can then establish historically that in the East under the influence of Alexandria the resurrection has for the first time acquired independence with regard to the death as is evidenced by the results of those that calculated the date of Easter and the re-organization of the worship in the fourth century.[29] In other words, the community is the centre in the *pascha-transitus* tradition, more than in the *pascha-passio* one: mindful of the Lord's *transitus* it carries out its own *transitus* from the old life to the new. This new life dawns, so to speak, from the pole of the resurrection. The community is on the move and as such applies to itself the paschal liberation of the Lord. But it seems to me that this spirituality of being on the way has had still another consequence beyond seeing the resurrection in its own light and emphasizing it. It also led the way towards the gradual incorporation of the initiation in the framework of the Easter night celebration. For this event is pre-eminently the ritual *transitus*. First, baptism is the Christian presentation of the Old Testament typology of the passage through the Red Sea. But it also counts as the neophyte's ritual enactment of Jesus' death and resurrection. Then it is the liturgical service in which man passes from the old to the new, the change of turning away from evil and turning towards the Lord. Against this background one can see that Easter day came to be the outstanding day for baptism and that baptism came to be related to the Easter celebration itself. There are too few exact data to see how precisely this came about but I assume that the initiation of adults did not take place during the celebration and in the presence of the community. For reasons of decency this took place elsewhere, in the baptistery. But we do know, for example, that the neophytes took part in the prayers and the Easter eucharist.[30] The initiation only became part of the Easter celebration in the true sense of the word under the influence of infant-baptism. This development reinforced the *transitus* character of the celebration. Although in the case of Asterius, for instance, we have still to do with a celebration which was totally paschal, so that it also included the *passio* aspect, one finds that in many liturgical traditions baptism has helped to shape the theme of the Easter celebration as is shown by, for instance, the reading schemes.[31] We can also refer to the initiation elements which marked the classic Western Lent of forty days. In conclusion, we may say that the integration of the initiation in the celebration has brought out and strengthened its *transitus* character.

From what has been said so far it is possible to deduce that through the influence of the *pascha-transitus* tradition the Easter celebration began to show the features of a 'rite of passage'. According to Van Gennep, a rite of passage is determined by two poles, one of departure and one of arrival, one representing the old phase of life or situation and the other the new.[32] It is also essential for a passage rite that the distance between the two poles is covered ritually, in such a way that the rites fill in the no man's land between the two and make it possible to pass over from one pole to the other by a separating process with regard to the first and a 'drawing-nearer', uniting process with regard to the second. In this sense the Easter celebration never was merely a passage rite, nor did it remain totally different from it. Particularly the nocturnal context of the celebration and the built-in initiation ritual have in their own way contributed to the passage character. Yet, it seems to me that this was a secondary matter: of far deeper importance for the paschal experience and liturgy was the early separation made between Good Friday and Easter Sunday which in essence and beforehand precluded the meaning and process of a passage.

But if, because of unfortunate historical circumstances, the Easter celebration could not grow into a passage rite or at the most only accidentally through the influence of a lively *pascha-transitus* tradition, is it then meaningful to resume the historical development and to work out in our own way the expansion of the celebration into a passage rite? It would seem that, within the scope of this article, the answer to this question depends on the theological value which one attaches to the tradition of the *pascha-transitus* as such. Can we theologically attach such a relevance to the core of this tradition that this core enables us to celebrate the Lord's Pascha? The answer is difficult but it seems to me that it must be negative for two reasons. First of all, because the *pascha-transitus* tradition seems to start in principle from the polar duality of death and resurrection, and I am convinced that, because of the theological observations made above, this is no longer possible with one single meaning. By putting Jesus' death and his resurrection next to, or over against, each other as two poles, even in their reciprocity, one understands them as two comparable events of salvation which would in themselves show equal features on the level of their historicity and their effectiveness for salvation. On this point reference to present-day Christology must suffice.[33] But it is particularly thinking about the various factors mentioned in this article which convinced me that the original Christian celebration of Easter during the night—especially this night—was in essence not so much meant to be the execution of a *transitus,* a change-over, as a watching with and for the Lord. It is a night of reflection, with the great witness of Scripture in hand and heart. It is a night during which we identify with the story of Jesus Christ, Lord of the new life out of the chaos of his death. It is a night of intense believing trust in the events of his life, in the hope of the eschatological working out of his life in us, our world, our time. It is a night of intense silence—a subdued yet exciting silence—in which one listens to stories which, without exception, relate how, under the guidance of a Saviour-God, resurrection comes about out of complete ruin and disaster. It is a night when no believer shuns the passion and does not need to shun it because it is the night of Jesus our Lord. To me the Easter celebration has more the character of contemplation than of action; it is pre-eminently a watch during the depth of night, not the expulsion of darkness; it is an acceptance of the darkness—Jesus' passion—through (and not: after) which light dawns—his resurrection. In conclusion I find that the *pascha-passio* is the older, and not only for the beginning but hopefully also for the future.

The foregoing does not imply that there is no room for passage rites in Christian worship. They will be necessary, also for the believer in our present time. I only tried to show that the Easter celebration has a peculiar character of its own as vigil for the Lord. I also feel that, in whatever Christian passage rite, the key motif of the Easter liturgy must be there where the life of the individual believer and the community is lived. In this sense, too, Easter is the feast of feasts.

CONCLUSION

The study of the original Christian celebration of Easter prompts the demand for a continual renewing.[34] The way in which the western liturgy gave shape to this shows a historical development which did not do justice to certain essential features, particularly the unity of the paschal mystery and the spirituality based on the passion of the Lord. The revision of the Easter celebration should concentrate on a theologically justified choice of the scriptural texts. It should start from the realization that the initiation elements are not necessarily a part of this celebration. It should attach great importance to the song of praise, which belongs to this night. It should create the atmosphere of a 'vigil', contemplation of the kind that becomes actuality in the Lord's Supper. Simplicity of form and a joyful but subdued disposition are factors which ensure a genuine celebration of Jesus' Pasch. This starts from the readiness of the community to accept this night indeed as a watch in and with the Lord.

Translated by Theo Westow

Notes

1. 'Art und Sinn der ältesten christlichen Osterfeier', in *Jahrbuch f. Liturgiewissenschaft*, 14 (1934), pp. 1–78.

2. *Ordo Sabbati Sancti, quando vigilia paschalis instaurata peragitur* (Typis polygl. Vat. 1952). *Dominica Paschae in Resurrectione Domini, Vigilia paschalis, Missale Romanum* (Typis polygl. Vat. 1970), pp. 266–88.

3. A. van Gennep, *Les rites de passage* (Mouton, Paris, 1909, repr. 1969).

4. C. Mohrmann, *Etudes sur le latin des chrétiens* (Rome, 1958), pp. 205–22.

5. B. Botte, 'La question pascale: Pâque du vendredi ou Pâque du dimanche?' in *La Maison-Dieu* 41 (1955), pp. 84–95. W. Huber, *Passa und Ostern* (Berlin, 1969).

6. M. Richard, 'La question pascale au IIe siècle', in *L'Orient Syrien* 6 (1961), pp. 179–212.

7. W. Cadman, 'The Christian Pascha and the Day of the Crucifixion, Nisan 14 or 15?' in *Studia Patristica* V, *Texte u. Unters.* 80 (Berlin, 1962), pp. 8–16.

8. B. Botte, art. cit., pp. 86–90.

9. M. Richard, art. cit., pp. 182–88.

10. B. Botte, art. cit., pp. 92–93.

11. B. Botte, 'Préface', in O. Casel, 'La fête de Pâques dans l'église des Pères', in *Lex Orandi* 37 (Paris, 1963), pp. 7–10.

12. R. Cantalamessa, *L'omelia 'in S. Pascha' dello Pseudo-Ippolito di Roma* (Milan, 1967). J. Fontaine and C. Kannengiesser, 'Les homélies pascales de Méliton de Sardes et du Pseudo-Hippolyte et les extraits de Théodote', in *Epektaxis* (Paris, 1972), pp. 263–71.

13. G. Kretschmar, 'Christliches Pascha im 2. Jahrhundert und die Ausbildung der christlichen Theologie', in *Recherches d. Sc. Rel.*, 60 (1972), pp. 287–323.

14. B. Botte, 'Pascha', in *L'Orient Syrien*, 8 (1963), pp. 213–26.

15. C. Mohrmann, 'Pascha, passio, transitus', op. cit., p. 215.

16. B. Botte, 'Préface', p. 10.

17. B. Courtoyer, 'L'Origine égyptienne du mot "Pâque"', in *Rev. Bibl.*, 62 (1955), pp. 481–96.

18. C. Mohrmann, op. cit., pp. 216–22.

19. W. Huber, op. cit., pp. 148–208.

20. G. Kretschmar, art. cit., p. 312.

21. C. Mohrmann, op. cit., p. 220.

22. R. Cantalamessa, op. cit., pp. 282–333.

23. H. Auf der Maur, *Die Osterhomilien des Asterios Sophistes* (Trier, 1967), pp. 37–63.

24. C. Mohrmann, op. cit., pp. 216–7.

25. H. Auf der Maur, op. cit., pp. 63–70 and 102–25.

26. C. Mohrmann, op. cit., p. 219.

27. H. Auf der Maur, op. cit., pp. 112–6.

28. R. Bornert, *Les commentaires byzantins de la divine liturgie du VIIe au XVe siècle* (Paris, 1966), pp. 52–72.

29. V. Loi, 'Il 25. marzo dato pasquale e la chronologia giovannea della passione in età patristica', in *Ephem. Lit.* 85 (1971), pp. 48–69.

30. G. Winkler, 'Einige Randbemerkungen zum osterlichen Gottesdienst in Jerusalem von 4. bis 8. Jahrhundert', in *Orient. Christ. Per.*, 39 (1973), pp. 481–90.

31. B. Kleinheyer, 'Haec nox est', in *Lit. Jahrbuch* 21 (1971), pp. 8–9.

32. A. van Gennep, op. cit., pp. 13–5. See J.-Y. Hameline, 'Relire van Gennep . . . Les rites de passage', in *La Maison-Dieu*, 112 (1972), pp. 133–43.

33. E.g., E. Schillebeeckx, *Het verhaal van een levende* (Bloemendaal, 1974), pp. 223–445. Cf. A. Ziegenaus, 'Auferstehung im Tod: Das geeignetere Denkmodell?' in *Münch. Theol. Zeitschr.*, 28 (1977), pp. 109–32 (with neg. crit.).

34. On this point see: *Lit. Jahrbuch* 21 (1971), pp. 1–58 (B. Kleinheyer, H. Reifenberg, H. Vorgrimler, H. Auf der Maur & R. Berger).

Walter von Arx

The Churching of Women after Childbirth: History and Significance

BIRTH and death are basic natural phenomena. At all times and in all cultures, birth and death are experienced as very special events. The less men were able to comprehend the link between them, the more rituals and traditions grew up round these decisive milestones of existence. This was long before Christianity began to influence men's thought or faith. How did Christianity come to terms with these attitudes and traditions?

Through a study of birth or—to be more precise—the Church's attitude towards the mother after childbirth, this article will attempt to demonstrate how difficult it was for the Church to dismiss these deep-rooted ideas or to adapt them to Christianity. This was all the more complex with regard to the subject of birth because of its connection with sex. The latter was treated by most ancient civilizations as mysterious and filled with dubious powers. Influenced by Old Testament ideas and by a variety of philosophical attitudes, Christianity likewise adopted a negative outlook on everything connected with sex.[1]

This approach had an undeniable influence on church practice. However, apart from the exclusion of women from liturgical services there are really no discernible effects on the liturgy for the first thousand years of the church's existence. But from the eleventh century onwards a custom was included in liturgical books which was to have an increasing influence on life in the Church. Namely, the blessing of the mother the first time she attended church after giving birth to a child.

IMPURITY OF THE WOMEN AFTER CHILDBIRTH

Early in the history of the Church, women in childbirth were considered unworthy to enter the house of God until a certain time after they had given birth. This practice was due above all to the widespread superstition as well as to the Old Testament laws governing purity.

It was believed that while giving birth a woman is particularly exposed to the influence of demons.[2] This superstition also stated that even when she has given birth she is still impure and that any work she might do would bring disaster. Ploss and Bartels have documented that this concept of the impurity of the woman who had given birth is also widespread among primitive peoples and that in most cultures one can find customs marking the end of the period of childbirth.[3]

However, these widespread attitudes were not the sole reason for the Church adopting such an approach. This was due far more to the laws of the Old Testament. According to the law of Moses women were considered impure for seven days after the birth of a boy and for fourteen days after the birth of a girl. They were only permitted to enter the temple for purification after thirty-three or sixty-six days respectively (Lev 12: 1–8). This Jewish attitude was taken over by the oriental church where it became firmly established. After the birth a woman had to go to the church for purification.

This practice was not without consequences for the western church. The inferiority of bodily functions was emphasized in particular by the penitentials influenced by Graeco-Celtic thought. They prescribed that a woman must go through purification rituals before she may enter the church after the birth of a child.[4]

This attitude was subsequently transferred to the western church, though there is no ecclesiastical law stipulating purification. In several rituals it is stated explicitly: 'Nulla lege tenetur mulier abstinere, ullo die post partum, ab ingressu Ecclesiae'. This is a reference to Pope Gregory the Great (+ 604) who stated emphatically in a letter to the Archbishop of Canterbury that a woman was not committing any sin if she went to church to give thanks to God even the hour after giving birth.

In spite of this unequivocal statement the attitude persisted that women were impure. The rituals emphasized that this was not based on any law; nevertheless the custom was recommended, the tradition as approved by the church, that women go to church after giving birth.

THE CHURCHING OF WOMEN IN THE RITUALS

The rituals for this first visit to church are presented in several different formulations. The most customary are: 'Benedictio mulieris post partum' and 'Introductio mulieris post partum in Ecclesiam'. The first of these expressions is used for blessing the mother in her own home as well as in the church. The German word *Muttersegen* is of more recent origin; previously the most commonly used term was *Aussegnung*, a more general bestowal of blessing, which can lead to misunderstanding. The term adopted in French is *relevailles,* and in English 'churching'. In the Evangelical Church the terms 'churching' and 'consecration' predominate.[5]

The fact that the churching of women caused considerable difficulties to the compilers of church rituals can be seen from the way it has been incorporated into the rituals. Although it is a blessing the formula is invariably found in section dealing with the sacraments, following either the marriage ritual or the ritual of baptism.

(a) Survey of the Different Formulations

Since all the *manuscript rituals* are not available for research, it is impossible to establish with certainty when the ritual of the churching of women first started. We may, however, accept as valid Franz's statement that the first formulae date from the end of the eleventh century. In any event not one prayer for this purpose is to be found in any sacramentary, although they contain sundry benedictions, prayers and various votive masses commemorating birth and death: for example, personal votive masses for the date of birth.

It may seem surprising that the earliest known formulae date from as late as the eleventh century. Prior to this time, women did however have to wait for a certain length of time after the birth of a child before they went to church. But it appears that this first visit to church was not accompanied by any special liturgical celebration.

The emergence of a particular blessing for women after childbirth must be attributable to the notion of the ritual and moral impurity of the woman during the period of childbirth as propagated by the penitentials.

The formulae found in manuscripts and early printed books sometimes vary considerably.[6] All contain in some form the idea that the woman must undergo a process of purification after childbirth.

The *Rituale Romanum* issued in 1614 by Pope Paul V marks the first major step towards the liturgical structure of the blessing of the mother. Given the extent to which the notion of the uncleanliness of the mother held sway both in popular tradition and in liturgical books, one can support B. Fischer's praise of the *Rituale Romanum* when he states that it 'shows a nice sense of moderation and dignity in the way it recalls certain older forms while at the same time rejecting some medieval traditions. For example, it remains one of its claims to fame that for the first time the unfortunate traditional motif of purification was finally excluded from the blessing of the mother, the *Benedictio mulieris post partum*'.[7] In contrast to earlier texts the *Rituale Romanum* created a specifically New Testament ritual containing virtually no references to the Old Testament concept of purification.

One could summarize the 'Benedictio mulieris post partum' of the *Rituale Romanum* [8] as follows: The priest receives the mother, who kneels before the church doors holding a burning candle. He sprinkles her with holy water, pronounces the 'Adjutorium . . .', the antiphon 'Haec accipiet' and Psalm 23, 'Domini est terra'. With the call 'Ingredere in templum Dei, adora Filium Beatae Mariae Virginis; qui tibi foecunditatem tribuit prolis', he leads the mother into the church, putting the stole round her hand. She kneels in front of the altar. There follows the Kyrie, Pater noster, and a prayer. The priest then sprinkles the mother once more with holy water and blesses her.

While one may welcome the fact that diocesan rituals were allowed to retain their own particular rites despite the introduction of the *Rituale Romanum,* it is regrettable that the Roman book did not exert a greater influence on individual rites with regard to the churching of women. It was for this reason that the old idea of purification persisted in the liturgy until the rite eventually died out following Vatican II.

A comparison of the rite for the churching of women in all available rituals used in German-speaking countries and some important books from the neighbouring areas demonstrates that even when the *Rituale Romanum* was adopted previous rites—though in our eyes without any doubt worse—were also retained. Hence the notion that women are impure is found repeatedly in different rituals right up to the twentieth century. This is illustrated in the *Rituals of the Diocese of Augsburg.*

Studies of rituals by various authors have established that the *Rituale Romanum* was introduced with the Rituals of Augsburg in 1656. However, there is no indication of this in the formula for the churching of women which corresponds word for word to the ritual of 1612. This, in turn derives to a large extent from a book published in Augsburg in 1580, in which reference is made to 'days of purification'; it also contains the 'Aufer' and the prayer from Candlemass, 'purificata tibi mente'.

In the preface to the revised edition of 1688, the concordance with the Roman ritual is praised as a wonderful sign of the unity of the faith.

Nevertheless, the churching of women after childbirth still adheres completely to the Augsburg tradition. The formula of 1612 was copied verbatim. Similarly, the ensuing editions of 1691 and 1728 also contained the unchanged ritual. Only in 1764 can the influence of the *Rituale Romanum* be perceived for the first time. Yet the motif of purification is not completely removed, nor in the editions of 1835 and 1857. The ritual of 1870 finally took over the exact form of the *Rituale Romanum*. Two additions were made, but only in footnotes.

A similar development can be traced for the majority of dioceses. One of the first books containing the verbatim formula for the blessing of women after childbirth as given in the *Rituale Romanum* is the ritual of Mecheln dating from 1617, whereas in the diocese of Osnabrück it was only adopted in 1906.

It is understandable that the blessing of women after childbirth should come under fire from reformers in the Enlightenment and the first half of the nineteenth century. Church benedictions were especially affected by the new ideas. The Sacraments, in so far as they retained their validity at all, lost their significance as instruments of grace. Nevertheless, the rituals retained the churching of women, as can be seen from the formulae suggested. The reason for this was presumably that this custom was rooted so deeply in popular tradition that even the most radical reformer did not dare to dispense with it altogether. However rituals of the time do not contain allusions to the mother's need for purification. The rites are orientated towards thanksgiving and petition.

Following the revised edition of the *Rituale Romanum* in 1925, rituals in German-speaking countries have virtually adopted the Roman rituals. One exception is constituted by the *United Ritual for all German Dioceses* brought out in 1950. It contains a bilingual ritual for the blessing of women after childbirth which emphatically and unequivocally stresses the aspect of thanksgiving. This is achieved not the least by virtue of the fact that instead of a psalm the prayer included is the Magnificat.[9]

(b) The Motif of Purification in the Liturgical Formulae

Franz defines the liturgical formulae as follows: 'In the Latin Church the whole act has the character of thanksgiving and the petition to God that he might continue to provide protection for both body and soul. However, it also contains traces of the old notion that the woman who has just given birth is marked by a moral blemish'.[10]

If, however, one studies the motif of impurity in all available liturgical formulae from the earliest printed versions up to the beginning of this century, one is forced to reverse Franz's definition. Most of the books are permeated by the underlying thought of purification from blemish and sin. The motif of thanksgiving tends to fade into the background whereas the petition for God's protection for body and soul assumes the greater importance.[11]

Sometimes even the heading of the formula refers to impurity, as for example: 'De purificatione mulieris post partum' or 'Benedictio mulieris purificandae post partum'. The opening petition 'Aufer' and certain antiphons (e.g., 'Ne reminiscaris . . . delicta nostra') allude rather explicitly to the impurity of the woman who has recently given birth.

As regards the choice of psalms it is agreeably surprising to see that the psalm of contrition 'Miserere' (Psalm 50) which occurs regularly in the manuscript rituals is never used in the printed books. In the *Rituale Romanum*, Psalm 23 was chosen, which must be described as an error; a choice perhaps suggested by the underlying thought of the entry into the temple, though the expression 'innocens manibus et mundo corde' was presumably a decisive factor. This at any rate is what von Baruf-faldus claims.[12] Although Psalm 23 contains no explicit allusion to the impurity of women after childbirth it may have contributed indirectly to the fact that the 'misconception of the rite of atonement' [13] could not be overcome.

In his comments on the entry into the church when the priest's stole is laid on the mother's hand, Baruffaldus again demonstrates his incli-nation to believe in the woman's need for purification. The act of touching the stole symbolizes a protection against demonic influences and the woman is thus simultaneously worthy to enter the church once more.[14] The petitions also contain the idea of purification.

In addition to the liturgical texts themselves, the opening and closing rubrics and the footnotes often support the idea of a necessary purifica-tion of the mother. According to Baruffaldus, in being received by the priest at the door of the church the woman is openly showing her humility; that she is not worthy to enter the house of God because she is still impure.[15]

The interpretation of the churching of women as a purification from some moral blemish is demonstrated most tragically with regard to the mother who dies either during the birth or in the post-natal period. In some places such women, because they had not been 'blessed', were denied a church burial in the cemetery and they were buried instead outside the cemetery walls as if they were suicides. Several synods had to take steps against this practice.

And the custom of blessing a woman who had died in childbirth before she would be buried was fairly widespread. Here again, we find the underlying thought that a woman who died during or after childbirth without receiving the blessing could not enter into the presence of God. Indeed, in the sixteenth century there were formulae for blessing women who died in childbirth, and although only a few of these formulae have come down to us, the custom seems to have been fairly widespread. Eighteenth- and nineteenth-century rituals had to contain a directive stipulating that such women did not have to be blessed. The custom of substituting another woman for the ritual of being led into the church was also forbidden.

INTERPRETATION OF THE CHURCHING OF WOMEN

Beyond any doubt, in liturgical history the churching of women after childbirth is interpreted as an act of purification. But this is only to say that the compilers of a ritual or the church authorities who approved the books on the whole saw the blessing of mothers as a purification rite.

But this does not necessarily mean that the priest who administered the blessing or the woman who received it did so in that spirit. The texts were read in Latin which was understood by very few of the women. It also depended on how the priest interpreted the rite. Hence one should study the addresses found in some of the rituals,[16] as well as sermons and popular writings from this point of view.

In his interpretation the priest had to counteract the message of the liturgical formula in addition to popular feeling. Among the population in general the idea of the impurity of women after childbirth held sway incontestably—and can still be found occasionally today. The church had supported this approach for too long, owing to its negative attitude to everything physical. Whether consciously or unconsciously it was generally understood that after giving birth a woman was tainted by a certain blemish and thus could not go to church or receive the sacraments. Even today there are some older women who consider it a sin for a young mother to go to church again without being 'blessed'.

In contrast, an attempt was made to lend a Christian interpretation to the liturgical rite of churching the mother, with particular reference to the example of the Virgin Mary. 'Since Mary also submitted to this regulation it was felt that Christian women should follow suit . . . The church thus rejects the notion of atonement on the part of young mothers, but it does approve of copying the idea of Mary's visit to the temple to offer thanks and to present the child . . . If through ignorance or ill-will this blessing is stigmatized as an act of purification and is thus resented by Christian mothers, they should follow the example of Mary's humility and even allow themselves to be blessed when it is misunderstood and despised by others'.[17] Special emphasis is laid on those aspects that can be drawn from Mary's visit to the temple: thanksgiving, presentation of the child and petition for the blessing of God.

One other point of view should not be overlooked. At a time when no movements existed to protect the rights of women, the church's insistence of maintaining popular traditions also brought advantages to mothers. Throughout the centuries popular tradition would not permit a woman to leave the house after childbirth until she had received the blessing of the church. This provided an important protection for young mothers, especially in agricultural communities where every pair of hands was essential. Otherwise they would have had to return to hard labour in the fields a few days after giving birth. The church not infrequently extended the date for the mother's first attendance in church, often to as much as forty days in imitation of Mary's visit to the temple. In this way the liturgical blessing functioned as a means of sparing women for a while after childbirth.

THE CHURCHING OF WOMEN TODAY

The Church has always known how to absorb events in the human existence and popular customs into the liturgy. As is well known, it succeeded extremely well in taking over pagan festivals and translating them into the Christian context. This also applies to the way in which various forms of blessing indicate the influence of human customs on the liturgy.

Since Vatican II the attempt has been made to introduce a new understanding of the sacraments. To give one example, it will take a long time and a lot of patience before the new approach to the anointing of the sick becomes firmly rooted in the popular consciousness and this sacrament is really understood as a sacrament for the sick and not for the dying.

Instead of working towards a re-evaluation of the tradition of churching, another, more radical solution has been found. The compilers of the baptism ritual have simply dispensed with the blessing; that is, they have reduced it to one single petition incorporated into the rite of baptism.[18] The baptismal ceremony concludes with a blessing, which is first imparted to the mother carrying her newly-baptized infant in her arms. Presumably to avoid giving any preference to the mother in the new baptismal formula, in keeping with the contemporary equality of the sexes, this is immediately followed by a blessing for the father and for all those present.

It should be pointed out that a new German benedictional[19] contains specific blessings for the mother before and after the birth. In the introduction to the blessing of the mother after the birth it states: 'The baptismal rite concludes with a blessing for the mother, the father and all present. The blessing of the mother replaces the former tradition of churching. Should the mother not be able to be present at the baptism of her child, it is appropriate that she come to church with her recently-baptized child in order to thank God for the birth and to receive his blessing'.

The whole ritual is permeated by a feeling of happy praise and thanksgiving. The suggested readings are: Lk 2:22b–28, 39–40 (the presentation of Jesus in the temple) and 1 Sam 1:20–28 (Samuel is brought into the house of the Lord). These are followed by the Magnificat, two blessing prayers of one's choice and finally a solemn concluding blessing. However, for the time being this kind of blessing is only to be found in the German benedictional.

Was it right to abolish the independent ritual of churching in the course of the post-conciliar reform of the liturgy? There were clearly justifiable grounds for abolishing it. Although 350 years have elapsed since the *Rituale Romanum*, it has not been entirely possible to get rid of the attitude that mothers are in need of purification. In addition, the fact that churching has been practically unknown for decades, especially in cities, lent support to the idea of dropping it altogether.

The only thing in favour of retaining the ritual is tradition. Churching is after all a blessing which was contained in the rituals for almost a thousand years in a variety of different formulae, some of them very beautiful. The liturgy yielded to the mother in that it gave ceremonial form to her first visit to church after the birth and made it possible for her to thank God for the successful birth of her child in a liturgical celebration.

The most recent solution offers us the possibility that both churching and the un-Christian attitude that birth entails the impurity of the woman will be forgotten. This could lead to a situation a few decades from now where a specific blessing of the mother after giving birth would be introduced which would constitute a genuine act of thanksgiving not merely as a liturgical rite but as a popular custom.

Translated by Sarah Twohig

Notes

1. R. Kottje, 'Studien zum Einfluss des Alten Testamentes auf Recht und Liturgie des frühen Mittelalters (6.–8. Jh.)', in *Bonner Historische Forschungen,* 23 (Bonn, 1964), esp. pp. 69–83; M. Daly, *The Church and the Second Sex* (London, 1968).

2. P. Browe, 'Beiträge zur Sexualethik des Mittelalters', in *Breslauer Studien zur historischen Theologie,* 23 (Breslau, 1932), p. 15; cf. also D. Symoens,'Le sacral et la mentalité actuelle. Un exemple: les revailles, in *Paroisse et liturgie* (Bruges, 1966), pp. 690–701.

3. H. Ploss, M. & P. Bartels, *Das Weib in der Natur- und Völkerkunde* (Berlin, 1927), III, pp. 159–83.

4. Cf. in detail A. Franz, *Die kirchlichen Benediktionen im Mittelalter* (Freiburg-im-Br., 1909), III, pp. 214–23.

5. The Evangelical and Old Catholic Churches also have a tradition of churching the mother after birth.

6. The oldest texts have been assembled by A. Franz, op. cit., pp. 210–12; for more recent formulae, pp. 224–29.

7. B. Fischer, *'Das Rituale Romanum* (1614–1964). Die Schicksale eines liturgischen Buches, in *Trierer Theologischz Zeitschrift,* 73 (1964), pp. 260f.

8. *Rituale Romanum,* tit. VIII, cap. 6.

9. *Collectio rituum ad instar appendicis Ritualis Romani pro omnibus Germaniae Diocesibus* (Ratisbon, 1950), tit. IV, caput 4.

10. A. Franz, op. cit., p. 230.

11. In a short article, I cannot cite each liturgical source specifically. I must also forego precise details of the sources. I hope to be able to publish the most important texts in a more detailed study.

12. H. Baruffaldus, *Ad Rituale Romanum commentaria* (second ed., Venice, 1752) tit. 43, no. 35.

13. B. Fischer, 'Das Trierer Rituale im 19. Jahrundert. Ein Beitrag zur Geschichte der deutschen Diözesanritualien', in *Trierer Theologische Studien,* 15 (1962), p. 254.

14. A Baruffaldus, op. cit., tit. 43, no. 29.

15. A. Baruffaldus, op. cit., tit. 43, no. 23–24.

16. E.g., Trier 1836 and 1873.

17. A. Scherer, *Geweihte Mutterschaft. Vom Sinn und Bedeutung der Aussegnung* (Colmar, n.d.), pp. 9 & 11.

18. *Ordo baptismi parvulorum* (1969), nos. 70 and 247–8.

19. Cf. *Gottesdienst* 9 (1975), pp. 1–4.

Philippe Rouillard

The Liturgy of the Dead
as a Rite of Passage

EVERY major journey needs some preparation and guides for almost all destinations are available; similarly, parents or friends often accompany one to the station or airport. It is no different anywhere in the world when it comes to the last journey which all men have to make one day. In all ages and in all cultures custom and religions have developed 'instructions for passing over'—a rite of passage or a death ritual which concerns not only the traveller but his entourage.

Before talking about the Christian liturgy of death as a rite of passage—and that is the topic of the present article—we have to think about the way in which we mortals understand and celebrate this passage into death; this fact of a man leaving his friends, relatives and neighbours, quitting this world and departing for that place which, in relation to our stay on earth, we call the beyond or heaven. After this inquiry, which cannot be restricted to the fragment of territory which we know as contemporary Europe, we shall be in a position to see how the Roman liturgy, after meditation on the Jewish Exodus and Christ's Passover, ritualized and sacramentalized the passing over of a Christian by relating it to the mystery of salvation. This dual inquiry will lead to the conclusion that the human and Christian transition of death cannot be separated from those previous stages which, in the course of his existence, have initiated man into mystery and the possession of life.

Almost all cultures and religions have presented death as the start of a dangerous journey which, after several obstacles, ought to lead to a blessed rest or a deep sleep. For the Greeks, the dead man could reach the other world only after crossing the river Styx in Charon's boat, for which he paid an obolus as the ferryman's fee. Accordingly, the dead man's relatives would place an obolus in his mouth before burial.

African Rituals

In western Africa, death is not thought of as an insuperable barrier separating two worlds but as a transition which allows one to pass from the village of the living into the village of the ancestors. The African takes care to transform physical death into a ritual death. The numerous ceremonies and prayers which envelop death, burial and mourning mark this passage from one world to another. The close relations have to die symbolically with the dead man so that he is not alone on this dangerous road. They whiten their bodies with clay, eat raw food, shave their heads, take off their clothes, sleep on the ground and now on a mat, and enter the house of the dead for a short time: all these are symbolic gestures which stand for participation in death.[1]

In many ethnic communities in Africa, especially when a chief has died, the funeral ceremonies do not take place until several weeks or months after the actual physical death, which is followed by a preliminary burial. The village community needs time to get together the food necessary for the funeral celebration, but at a deeper level it is proper not to separate too soon from the chief who ruled the village for so many years. Time must also be found to choose his successor so that the village is not left without a guide. Finally, it is thought that the final ceremonies should not take place until the body has reached a skeletal state. Hence, biologically and sociologically, death is not an event at this or that point in time but a process which requires all the more time when the dead man played a major rôle in the community.

European Customs

To return to western Europe, and especially to France, we find in this area too an entire human and social ritual which sees death as a form of passage. This ritual is in the process of disappearing or changing, for various reasons: from the Christian viewpoint there is no longer any solid support in a largely de-Christianized society. The two wars of

1914–18 and 1939–45 increased the number of the dead to infinity and put an entire nation into mourning. The result was that an exceptional and unusual situation was generalized and became common. Finally, the development of urbanization, of motorized traffic, and of medical and hospital services, together with other factors of modernization, simultaneously brought a change in living conditions and conditions of dying. The way in which the last journey took place has changed almost as profoundly as other types of travel.

In the traditional system,[2] a man who feels that his end is approaching puts his affairs in order, completes or revises his will, says goodbye to his family and to his friends, and then dies at home, in the midst of family and acquaintances, in his familiar universe. As soon as he is dead, the family group carries out the ritual actions: makes an announcement to neighbours and relatives, prepares the body of the dead man, arranges the house and puts on mourning. The dead man is displayed on a catafalque or mourning bed, and for two or three days his friends and acquaintances file by in order to pay their last respects, as a gesture of separation.

On the day of burial, the dead man leaves his house, accompanied by all his relations and his friends, who have come again to escort him on his last journey. This slow funeral cortege is meticulously ordered and allows the dead man to pass for the last time through the rural or urban environment in which he lived.

The procession reaches the church, a necessary station on the road of the world beyond. At the church the dead man undergoes the ritual action which separates him from this world, provides the requisite purifications (holy water, incense, absolution) and supplies him with the recommendations which will make his entry to the life of the blessed easier. After the church stage, the procession leaves for the cemetery, to take the dead man to his 'last resting place'. The rites of burial and the earth thrown on the coffin mark a new point in the process of separation. But the flowers that gather on the grave, the more or less frequent visits to the graveyard, the celebration in Catholic countries of 2 November, show the family's attachment to its dead.

Before being able to resume normal life, and before being fully reintegrated in the world of the living, the close relations of the dead man will remain for a more or less extended period in a state which keeps them close to him and to death: mourning, with all its external signs (black clothing, withdrawal from social life, various taboos) represents the time and process necessary for the wound to heal and the conditions of everyday life to be re-established. This healing process is of variable length, depending on the degree of relationship with the dead man. For the widow, the healing process will never be at an end. She will remain in mourning and will bear its signs until she herself has rejoined her husband in death.

Throughout this summary account, one will easily recognize the three stages of any rite of passage: separation, intermediate situation, admittance. These phases apply both to the dead man and to the members of his family or group. The man who dies is cut off from the living but spends several days in a marginal situation before being buried and taking his place definitively among the dead. As for the family, the death of one of its members also cuts it off summarily from the normal human condition, and it is only after a more or less extended state of mourning that it can resume its place in the society of the living.

As we have already noted, the transformation in living conditions in the modern world has almost everywhere led to a corresponding change in the conditions of death. Hence it seems proper to spend some time on this new situation. But this work has already been carried out in certain regards.[3] Moreover, the new human death ritual remains pliable in a continuously changing world. For some years a considerable number of people have believed that man should recover the 'right to die' of which he is so often deprived by medical and hospital techniques. Beyond all change, however, there remains the inescapable reality of death together with the anguish of leaving a known for an unknown world; and the rupture brought about by separation, commencing a long process of healing and reintegration. What meaning does Christian liturgy propose in this regard?

THE CHRISTIAN DEATH RITUAL

Because the liturgy is oriented to man, and because the salvific gestures of Christ extended by Christian sacraments and rites have endowed the major events of man's individual or collective life with a new meaning and content, it was necessary to look at the human ritual of the last passage before coming to the Christian rites of death and burial.

My examination of Christian liturgy will be restricted to the Roman liturgy. I reluctantly abandon any treatment of the riches of the Eastern liturgies.[4] However, before approaching the ritual for the dead that has emerged from recent liturgical reforms, I shall look briefly at a few former stages in the development of the Roman rite for the dead, in order to show that once it was emphatically paschal in character, especially from the eighth century, and that this emphasis has been recovered to some extent in the present ritual.

The Roman Ritual of the Seventh Century

The oldest Roman ritual for death and burial is to be found in Ordo 49, which dates from the seventh century.[5] I shall outline the main characteristics of the rite, italicizing the Latin terms which refer to exit and entry. When the Christian is about to depart (*exitus*), he is given communion, which is a token of resurrection. The story of the Passion is read to him until the moment when his soul is about to leave (*egredere*) his body, when the response *Subvenite* is pronounced: 'Come, saints of God; advance, angels of the Lord . . .', and then Psalm 113 is recited, 'In *exitu* Israel', with the antiphon 'May the choir of angels receive you (*suscipere*)'. After death, the body is placed on a litter and carried in procession to the church. There no eucharist is celebrated but instead an office consisting of psalms is said, with a very expressive antiphon: 'May the angels lead (*ducere*) you into God's paradise, may the martyrs receive (*suscipere*) you on your arrival (*adventus*), and may they introduce (*perducere*) you into the holy city of Jerusalem'. A second procession takes the body from the church to the cemetery while Psalm 117 is recited, with the antiphon, 'Open the gates for me, and once I am within (*ingressus*) I shall praise the Lord'.

This ancient ritual which in one manuscript bears the significant title '*Incipit de migratione animae*',[6] is in fact a paschal transition ritual. Psalms 113 and 117, recited at the beginning and end of the liturgy, were part of the essential structure of the Jewish paschal meal. The Christian death celebration is the accomplishment of a paschal 'exodus': the dead person undergoes his exodus from Egypt, his liberation from exile, his entry into the Promised Land where he is received by angels and saints who come to meet him. The heavenly sojourn is presented in terms of the dual image of the garden (paradise) and the city (Jerusalem), which are symbols of the pleasure of life and of the security which are to be found in all oriental imagery of happiness.

The liturgical action consists for the most part of a procession with a recitation or chant which conducts the dead person from his earthly abode to the celestial Jerusalem, with one stage in the church, which is halfway between earth and heaven. Throughout this journey the Christian is not alone: at the start the earthly community accompanies him as far as it can, and on arrival he is welcomed by the inhabitants of heaven: that is, by those who have travelled before him (saints, martyrs and patriarchs), by the envoys of the master of the house (the angels), and finally by the master of the house in person. The dying Christian therefore passes from one community to another, and his 'transition' is related to Christ's Passion, either directly (the reading of the Passion), or more often indirectly by referring to the exodus and liberation of Israel. The death of each human being is trans-signified by its relation to the Passover of Christ, and is inserted into the great migration of all the people of God on the way towards the kingdom of heaven.

There is no space here to describe the further development of this ancient Roman ritual which, from the eighth century, changed the stress: a peaceful, paschal vision of Christian *transitus* was replaced gradually by a dramatic vision of judgment, a fraught discourse on the fate of this sinner who could get to heaven but who runs the risk of falling for ever into the fires of hell. God and his angels are no longer at the end of the road to welcome the dead person with open arms, but instead are there to examine him or to judge him before their tribunal: *Dies irae, dies illa!*

The New Rituals of Death and Burial

Today, after the liturgical reforms emanating from Vatican II, what discourse on death and the beyond, and what rites of passage and accompaniment are to be found in the new rituals? First we must ask where the answer to this question is to be sought, and therefore what rituals we have to consult. In the seventh century, the Roman death rite was addressed to a specific and relatively homogeneous society, with Latin as its means of expression. In the twentieth century, even though Christianity is to be found in every continent, a ritual published in Latin in Rome cannot be addressed to any specific society. It is a reference ritual, which is not intended to be used as such, but to be translated, transposed and adapted to different languages and local mentalities and customs. The authors of the Latin funeral rite have explicitly provided for this indispensable adaptation. On the other hand, after having inquired into the death and burial rituals of various countries, they have prepared three possible types of funeral liturgy, depending on whether the main celebration takes place in the home (the case in many parts of Africa), in the church (France and Italy), or at the cemetery (German-speaking Europe). There is no room to list all the many rituals which have been published or which are in preparation, and therefore I shall take as the reference work the Roman ritual which serves as inspiration for all the others.

But my study cannot rest content with the mere funeral ritual, which only takes effect after the death of the Christian. We have to begin with the ritual of the anoiting of the sick, which includes not only the sacrament of Extreme Unction but the rites of viaticum, possible confirmation in the case of danger of dying, and the commitment of the dying. There is reason to regret that for practical reasons the rites preceding death and those following it have been separated and divided into two. It would have been better to have had a single ritual for all successive yet continuous stages of the itinerary of a Christian passing from this world to the next. I hope this point will be taken into account by those responsible for developing a death and funeral ritual for their own countries.

Nevertheless, I shall try to show how the present Roman liturgy includes and celebrates the *transitus* of the Christian, taking into account the recommendation of Vatican II that the funeral rite should more obviously express the paschal character of Christian death and better respond to the situations and traditions of each area, even in liturgical colours.[7]

(a) *Leaving life*. A man who is about to die almost always feel abandoned, isolated, alone. Sickness, accident or old age have excluded him from the active life led by others, and he desires someone to be present and to hear something. The pastoral liturgy tries to cancel this solitude in various ways. On the one hand, it recommends pastors to visit the sick and in this way to show them that they are not cut off from and abandoned by the world. On the other hand, the sacrament of Extreme Unction, when administered to a man who is about to die, is intended to fill him with the power of the Spirit before that last battle which is beyond human power, and with regard to the resurrection and spiritualization to which he is called in the world beyond. But God's action takes place by means of human gestures which also have their own value: the laying-on of hands, the anointing with oil, answer the need which the sick person has for physical contact and a reassuring touch. We know how the sick, and of course the dying, ask those with them to hold their hand. This physical contact with a person who is lucky enough to be in good health seems a token of something contrary to weakness and isolation of the dying.

Before leaving this world, the Christian has to receive viaticum, that is, the Body of Christ, which is given as food for the journey. At times a quasi-magical value has been attributed to this viaticum and the Host has even been put into the mouths of the dead, rather as if it were the Greek obolus. In fact this last eucharist is intended to allow the Christian to integrate his own passage with the Passion and Resurrection of Christ, and also to give him that inward presence which, if it is really received, goes much further than human presence.

A last rite is provided for: in the last ritual it was known as 'recommendation of the soul', whereas the new ritual, having revised its anthropology in this regard, calls it 'recommendation of the dying person'. As far as the priest and those round about are concerned, it is a question of accompanying the dead man until his last moments and of creating a climate of prayer about him: the living are trying to help the dying person to remain in control of himself in the face of death. They recommend him to God who made him and recite at his bedside, or help him to say, the most ordinary prayers, the prayers of his youth. This latter concern corresponds to the need to return to the origins, to the safety of early infancy, which so often appears on the approach of death.

(b) *From one world to the other.* Inspired by traditional theology, the Roman burial ritual looks on death as separation of the soul and the body. After death, a dual journey begins for the dead person—that of his body and that of his soul, which will never be reunited until the day of resurrection which lies a long way off.

At the moment of death, the soul leaves the body and begins a 'migration' which takes it through the gates of death and should lead it to the gates of life. The ritual has retained the traditional imagery of gates: the gates of death (167), the gates of paradise (48), the gates of life (169). Before reaching heaven, the soul has to undergo divine judgment (46); it has to be liberated from mortality (172) and the last traces of its imperfections (193). But this theme of judgment is not heavily stressed. At the end of its journey the soul enters heaven, which is the place of peace and light (33, 53, 169), the company of angels and saints (46, 56, 193, 196), the bosom of Abraham (174), the house of God (117). The new ritual deliberately avoids any mention of purgatory, hell and Satan.

If the soul of the dead person is entrusted to the hands of God, his body is given into the hands of men, who have the duty of burying it (46): that is, of putting it in the earth so that it returns to the place from which it was drawn (55, 184). While allowing burial or cremation, the Church indicates its preference for burial, which increases 'hope in resurrection', or at least has more meaning in a Western civilization which is more sensitive to the symbolism of earth than to the symbolism of fire.

In this passage from one world to another, the new ritual has made an innovation by replacing the ancient rite of absolution (which was an intercession and a request for absolution) with a 'last recommendation' and a 'last farewell', which normally take place at the end of the celebration. This rite is the last stage of separation, the last gesture or last cry before the disappearance of the dead person.

(c) *Recovering life.* In the Christian ritual, the funeral liturgy remains unfinished. The *transitus* does not end with burial. The body is put into the earth, or less significantly into a stone or concrete vault which is supposed to protect it so that it may rise again on resurrection day. The soul has been entrusted to God because it awaits the day when it will once again enliven its own body. It is only on the 'last day' that the dead man will reach the end of his journey and, now fully human, rise again for eternal life.

The funeral rite does not speak of the beyond other than circumspectly. It keeps as far as possible to biblical phrases which are only metaphorical, and it obviously hesitates between an immediate eschatology and a nuanced eschatology by acknowledging that our categories of time and duration are not transferable to the other world. One affirmation recurs constantly: to enter heaven is to enter the assembly of saints and the blessed, to become one of the society of the elect. Certainly eternal life consists in being in the presence of God, of living in his light, but the vision of God, which later theology was to make the essence of blessedness, is not generally presented by the liturgy other than in the framework of the heavenly *ecclesia*. A careful examination of the new ritual shows that there are two superimposed layers, two series of texts with varying inspiration and orientation. Whereas the ancient prayers rarely mention Christ and entrust the dead man to God who will welcome him into the company of the saints, the new prayers composed for the revision of the ritual regularly refer to the paschal mystery and express a more individual eschatology.

CONCLUSION

The modern world tries to elude death in every possible way. It is agreed that the dying man should not know that he is going to die; that the presence and transit of bodies should not affect the peace and concerns of the living; that the signs of death and mourning should be hidden. Contrary to this dehumanizing tendency, the Christian liturgy takes pains to declare loudly and intelligibly the reality and meaning of this last passage: the dying Christian does not fade into mist but is carrying out one of the major tasks of his human existence. The ritual is intended to help the dying man to live his death as a man and as a believer, and it is intended to help his family to see the luminous aspect of Christian *transitus*. Experience shows that, in an atmosphere of faith, it is possible to celebrate truly paschal funeral services which show the meaning of the Christian pasch as well as Christ's passover.

One of the most positive elements of the new ritual is its presentation of a Christian's death as the last stage of an initiation which began at his baptism. The sacraments of Christian initiation find their equivalent in the sacraments or rites of the last anointing, viaticum and the funeral. The initial immersion is continued in the final burial, which is itself only a passing over. On several occasions the Roman ritual of death refers to baptism and meditates on the connexion between sacramental life and eternal life. It is by means of a series of passages and initiations that man enters into life, and it is by virtue of a succession of sacramental passages that the Christian gradually leaves the regions of darkness in order to proceed to the country of light.

Translated by John Griffiths

Notes

1. These indications are taken in part from a lecture given in Rome in February 1977 by J. F. Thiel, editor of the German journal *Anthropos*. In the course of a recent visit to western Africa I was able to confirm the finding that accompaniment of the dead is not always symbolic. When a chief dies companions have to be found for the journey. On the theme of death in Africa, see L.-V. Thomas & R. Luneau, *La Terre Africaine et ses Religions* (Paris, 1975), pp. 246–61, and R. Jaulin, *La Mort Sara* (in regard to Tchad) (Paris, second ed., 1971).

2. For a detailed account, see A. Van Gennep, *Manuel de Folklore Francais Contemporain*, I, 2 (Paris, 1946), pp. 649–824.

3. Cf. P. Ariès, *Essais sur l'Histoire de la Mort en Occident du Moyen Age à nos Jours* (Paris, 1975), pp. 157–63, 164–97; J. Potel, *Les Funérailles: une Fête* (Paris, 1973).

4. See P. Kovalevsky, 'Les funérailles selon le rite de Pâques et les prières pour les morts pendant le temps de Pâques à l'Ascension' (in the Byzantine liturgy) in *La Maladie et la Mort du Chrétien dans la Liturgie* (Rome, 1975), pp. 141–54; D. Webb, 'La liturgie des funérailles dans l'Eglise nestorienne', op. cit., pp. 415–32.

5. M. Andrieu, *Les Ordines Romani du haut Moyen-Âge*, IV (Louvain, 1956), pp. 523–30.

6. Ms Berol, Phillips 1667 (fol. 173), quoted by M. Andrieu, op. cit., p. 525.

7. *Constitution on the Liturgy* (Vatican II), art. 81.

PART III

Theological Reflections

Dionisio Borobio

The 'Four Sacraments' of Popular Religiosity: A Critique

THERE are many standpoints from which one could approach the subject of 'popular religiosity',[1] and several possible methods. I propose here to concentrate on a particular aspect: the sacramental nature of the central moments of the life-cycle,[2] and to adopt a particular method: that of evaluative analysis of the evidence based on anthropological, theological and pastoral criteria.[3] My approach is also a definite one: a critical approach, which supposes that it in its turn is open to criticism. This definition itself requires some hermeneutical clarifications, in view of the breadth of meaning covered by the title of the article and its thematic implications.

Writers who have dealt with the subject have usually limited its application in various ways: the religiosity of the 'rites of passage' (A. Van Gennep), 'the Catholicism of critical moments' (M. Mauss), 'festive Catholicism' (R. Pannet), 'the Catholicism of the four seasons of life' (J.-Y. Hameline), 'sacramental popular religiosity' (R. Vidales), 'celebrations of life and death' (F. Urbina), 'cultual religion of life cycles' (L. Maldonado). I find it preferable to speak of 'sacramental religiosity', since if by the term 'religiosity' one means the manner in which the great majority of the people—as distinct from the 'practising' minority—live their religious mediations, calling it 'sacramental' indicates that one is dealing with the basic mediations the Church proposes to the baptized.

Why, however, speak of 'four sacraments' of popular religiosity? What are these four sacraments? A point of clarification first: it is not that these Christians ask only for four sacraments, but that they generally ask for the sacraments only at four moments in in their lives. They do not ask for the traditional number to be reduced (they ask for confession at the time of first communion, and the eucharist at the time of matrimony), but their request is limited chronologically (to the four decisive and irreversible stages of life). Nonetheless, speaking of 'four sacraments' supposes not only a terminological choice, but also a preference of content, depending on the valorative criteria one adopts. There are, however, adequate reasons—ecclesiastical (the sacramental 'minimum' required by the Church for calling oneself a Christian), sociological (the sacraments normally asked for), and vital (the moments in the life cycle when they are asked for: birth, growing-up, marriage and death)—for defining the 'four sacraments' of popular religiosity as child baptism, first communion, matrimony and the last rites (with a mass). There is a perceptible synchronism between the decisive stages of life, man's tendency to sacralize these stages by means of the so-called 'rites of passage', and the petition (subject)— administration (Church) of these four sacraments of popular religiosity.

The subjects of this 'sacramental religiosity' are, therefore, those who have been baptized but do not 'practise' as a general rule, who cling to a religious belief imbued with socio-cultural catholicism, and usually express it at the decisive moments of the life-cycle, by means of the sacraments the Church offers and requires at these moments, as visible signs of their belonging to a socio-religious system.

APPROACH TO THE REALITY

Neither the religion nor the sacramental religiosity of the people are dead; they live on, as man and the people do, because man lives in the people. But, like man and the people, they are going through a period of deep crisis. This crisis cannot be solved through either exalting it romantically or setting it aside without due consideration. The first step needed is to recognize the complexity of the reality, singling out the attitudes displayed by the subjects and the most important causes of the crisis.[4]

(a) The Most Important Causes of the Crisis

The *challenge of secularism* has been and still is, I believe, one of the main causes of the crisis. Modern 'humanism', the technical-scientific mentality and the great social revolutions that unleashed the secularizing process, have not succeeded—as Compte, Marx, Weber and others prophesied they would—in bringing about the disappearance of religion. But they have brought about a crisis in religious culture and civilization, with a gradual erosion of the social systems that 'protected' a stabilizing and all-embracing religiosity; they have caused the 'death' of a particular image of God, man and the world. The birth of new religious-tinged phenomena and movements—counter-culture, esoterism, Jesus-movements or whatever one calls them—, though taken by some (Harvey Cox, Douglas Brown, R. Belloch, Roszak, A. Watts) as proof that 'God is not dead', or that religion persists despite the precipitate affirmations of the secularists (as claimed by Andrew Greeley, Gregory Baum, Joan Brothers . . .), has not produced anything that can be taken as a vital alternative to the crisis of religion, although some (such as Theodore Luckman and Andrew Greeley) would see them doing so in the future).[5] What has been proved once more, however, is that man cannot live without magic, without myths and rites, without mystery or religion, without nature and without senses. What is clear, too, is that the secularizing process has brought about a crisis in people's understanding of the sacramental mediations of the Church and their attitude to them. Once understanding of these has been broken down, their forms of expression tend to decay as well. When religion is 'de-churchified', faith in the religious system tends to be shaken too.

Many of the Catholics who belong to the mass of those who observe 'sacramental religiosity' no longer ask for the sacraments in order to protect themselves against mysterious or occult forces, to win a reward or escape divine retribution, to express their resignation in the face of the evils of the world and society, or to submit to a socio-political system that imposes such behaviour. Many say that the sacraments mean nothing to them, that they are no use. Their world speaks another language, and uses different signs. Their immediate problems and hopes are in another realm. Religious institutions are no longer the sole guardians of religious practice and ceremonial; so, here and there in the very heart of the secularized world, new religious forms are born or revived, new sacral mediations, new symbols—social, erotic, sporting or archaic—which despite their ambivalence seem to express man's religious dimension, the ideals to which he aspires. In not a few cases it would seem that the people have projected their liberating hope on to other, new 'sacraments of salvation', easier to understand and more effective, in the spheres of political and social life.

Clearly the people as such, with the exception of certain groups, are not conscious of this religious involvement, but yet feel drawn to it (particularly the young), with resulting effects on their behaviour toward the established system of religion, especially with regard to the sacraments. Whereas a minority abandon sacramental religiosity, the great majority accept it out of a mixture of resignation and frustration, and others experience it as a valid response to sacralization of the great steps in life.

So these questions emerge: will some forms be completely replaced by others? [6] What attitude should the Church take to sacramental religiosity if it is to answer the challenge of secularism? How can a people's sacramental religiosity, experienced in new situations, be given an adequate symbolic expression?

A second main cause of the crisis would seem to be the *inadequate response of the Church and Christians* to the problems of sacramental religiosity. Liturgical reform in the Church has had many positive aspects, but its application has been seriously deficient in many ways. In most cases, the adaptation of the reforms needed to suit them to different cultures and peoples has not even been minimally carried out.[7] The sacramental pastoral endeavour that should have been put into development of popular religiosity has often been halted in mid-stream through being wrongly conceived, for lack of means, from lack of perseverance and discouragement, if not from contrary views and antagonisms among those responsible for the pastoral endeavour itself.

The sufferers from all this are the people, the masses whose religious feelings are sacramental, since while, on one hand, their past mentality and 'sacramental' mediations have not been taken sufficiently seriously, on the other, their present 'sacramental' sensibility and mediations have not been accepted or valued properly either. A popular rite can only retain its vigour and meaning when it can combine the freshness of creativity with the original strength of the archetype. It is perhaps because this has not been achieved that our sacramental celebrations now fail either to please the old or to satisfy the young. This is the more serious in view of the marked tendency apparent today to reduce all mediation to exclusively sacramental forms. If the sacraments have always been the centre of popular religiosity, today they are often the last, and necessary, bastion in which this religiosity can express itself within the institution of the Church. It is not surprising, then, that given this sort of de-angelicization of the sacraments and the poverty of other forms of mediation, other ways should be sought, such as the privatization of religious expression within the confines of the individual and the family, and the sacramentalization of the secular in the political and public spheres.

If all this corresponds at least to a part of the reality of the situation, we need to ask ourselves how liturgical reform can be carried on in such a way that it overcomes destructive and one-sided attitudes, so as to arrive at a better understanding of and lead to an improvement in the sacramental religiosity of the people. What theological principles and pastoral 'strategies' can show the way to a solution of the problem?[8]

(b) The Most Significant Attitudes of the Subjects

The crisis of sacramental religiosity shows that it can undergo major changes over a long or medium space of time, but there is nothing to indicate its eventual disappearance. Despite everything, the bulk of Christians go on asking for the sacraments 'of life and death'. Why? What do they look for, hope for, seek to express in the sacraments?

In the first place, they are demonstrating their *need for rites*. Not profane or secular rites, but sacred rites, those rites whose existence is rooted in the tradition and religious culture of the people while at the same time referring them to a transcendent reality, through a 'reassuring' religious institution, above all human or technical manipulation. Neither the villager nor the city-dweller can live without rites. The religious foundation—or, as Hugo Assmann calls it, the 'Christian ideological surplus' [9]—has not died in the city, and tends to express itself almost irresistibly at the culminating moments of the life cycle. There is something lacking, something out of place, if 'the rites are not performed' at birth, marriage and death. Whether their rightful place in the sacramental order is understood or not, there is no doubt that they serve as the means of expression—as R. Pannet has pointed out—for many valuable aspirations that demand the presence of the supreme archetype [10], and for an opening-out to mystery, a self-offering and consecratory desire, a wish for communication between the divine and the human; all these are hard to repress at the decisive moments of life.

A rite is like an obligatory show at the fair, the basic reason for the festivity, the religious motive for summoning family and friends. Even if the celebration of the rite is dull and boring, individualistic or passive; even if the real feast precedes it or follows it, it is always considered an integral element of the feast by such Christians, and even as the reason for the feast. The sacramental rites are not the celebration, but they are part of it to the extent that they allow people to expand and express themselves, to enjoy themselves and relax, to affirm their being and strengthen their appreciation of it—from its deepest aspects, beyond the everyday routine—in rites that they may only be able to follow in silence, or admire with a greater or lesser degree of emotion. This may be one of the reasons why such Christians find rites necessary for a celebration to be complete, even though they do not see the sacramental rites as a celebration in themselves.

In the second place, people seek to express their religious *belief* and *hope*. Ritual is word and action, active word or eloquent action. It suggests more than it says, makes one think rather than expressing one's thoughts. It gives more indication of what one hopes for than of what one already has. Its language operates not on a rational or intellectual, logical or descriptive level, but on a trans-rational, emotional, experimental and sensitive one. This is why the Christian of popular religiosity loves rites. He tries to express his 'faith' through them, saying more than he knows how. His presence at them is his greatest eloquence; it indicates an attitude of openness to the divine, the transcendental, the unconditional, the mysterious. One cannot always be sure that such a reality will take the shape of the God of Our Lord Jesus Christ. In any case, for many people, 'believing' is just feeling themselves to be Catholic. Their faith is only in 'the faith of the Church', not a personal faith. This faith makes a man *hope for* something from rites. What he hopes for is basically to consecrate that moment to God, to win blessing and protection from God, to conjure away the dangers of a change of life, and to insure his future against threats of destruction and failure in this uncertain world. Recourse to God in these rites is not a spiritural luxury or pure devotion, but because God is necessary to prevent death, because life must be asserted over death. In many cases, this hope is clearly not free from 'magical', fatalistic or alienating attitudes. But, equally clearly, it shows a spirit of offering and acceptance, of vocation and in-vocation, a wish to place our realities and hopes in God's sphere, and this is not to be despised. In this way, the faith-hope expressed in sacramental religiosity is a 'trans-rationality that sows meanings in time, that makes and orientates history. What is impossible to known forces and the prognostications of science, is possible to God's power'.[11]

In the third place, people look for their *Christian identity and sense of belonging to a socio-religious system.* The sacramental rites are not only a way of celebrating life and expressing faith and hope, but also a means of integrating life in a process of religious socialization, a way of expressing how one wants to be 'religiously' in the world, a qualified means of saying that one is Catholic and Christian and not something else. To question this identity is often to wound these people in the very depth of their consciousness. Being Christian, for them, is above all wanting to be so. They are not concerned with dogmatic questions, nor moral requirements, nor the contradiction between 'their faith' and their lives. No more are they bothered by confessional or inter-Church differences. They have been baptized: this makes them Christians. And their right to receive the sacraments seems to them indisputable, whatever their motives. Sacramentalization is the institutional channel that best expresses and defines their belonging to a socio-religious system. They may not know the theological reasons for this belonging, but they are often more certain of it as a fact than other Christians. And yet they see the difference between themselves and 'unbelievers' on one side, and those who 'are always going to mass', or are 'stuck in Church' on the other.[12]

AN ANTHROPOLOGICAL INTERPRETATION

The anthropological interpretation of sacramental religiosity supposes an attempt to answer the question of whether this religiosity helps or hinders a true realization of the human ideal. Is sacramental religiosity the result of a simple accommodation to or acceptance of a cultural religious-symbolic system of belonging? What aspects of it can be accepted or rejected without mutilating or denying a basic human dimension? Does the present sacramental structure of the Church help man's self-realization?

To start with, we can say that sacramental religiosity is a form of *realization of the symbolic dimension of the human condition.* 'From our understanding of man as a being capable of infinitely surpassing himself and so forming the primary source of any symbolizing process, popular religiosity that creates, stimulates and re-vitalizes this symbolic capability, can only be seen as one of the most appropriate means of helping man to reach the heights of his ideals', provided two dangers are avoided: that of making use of his symbolic capability in a repressive or limiting way, and that of letting this capacity lead to an evasion of reality.[13] Man is a symbolical being and leads his existence symbolically. Sacramental symbols, rather than something imposed on man from outside, are something that responds to an inner need, the possibility of relating to the world, other men, and God.[14] Depriving man of the sacramental religiosity of these symbols would be fatally wounding to his very religious dimension, on the symbolical expression of which his personal self-realization depends.

Furthermore, the sacraments of popular religiosity respond to the almost vital need man has to *sacralize the decisive moments of his life-cycle.* However much one calls this correspondence pre-Christian (proper to pagan religions) and therefore non-theological, and even though one can show that Christ did not institute the sacraments for this purpose, it remains certain that such a correspondence evidences an anthropological fact that cannot be avoided. So, is it justifiable or desirable for the Church to situate the sacraments at these junctures of life? I believe it is.

As I see it, all the sacraments, in their own way, respond to basic situations in human life, which are at once sources of anthropological rooting and 'figures' of divine transcendence. These situations may or may not coincide with the biological times of transition, but they should always coincide with the anthropological times of 'calling'. The biological is an aspect of the anthropological, just as the anthropological in a dimension of the sacramental. These are correlated realities, referring one to another, not contradictory or mutually exclusive. A sacrament, the more it is inserted into these situations and embraces them in all their aspects, the better it shows its fullness of meaning and 'theandric' richness.[15] In some sense, all sacraments are sacraments of transition. But strictly speaking, only those that coincide with a biological transition also become rites of passage.[16] Some sacraments have a substratum of biological transition—birth = baptism; growth = first communion and confirmation; procreation = matrimony; sickness and death = last rites. Some indicate a change of state more clearly—from single to married = matrimony; from guilty to innocent—forgiven = penance; from lay to cleric = orders. All, finally, imply an anthropological situation and a paschal 'transition' in the mystery of Christ (the eucharist is the permanent source of transition in these situations and throughout the whole of life as a sign of the final eschatological transition). Therefore, while not strictly necessary, it is both valid and desirable for some sacraments to be brought out at times of biological transition.[17] What man seeks in his bio-anthropological autonomy and spontaneity becomes the basis for a free response, coming from the free will of God, through the sacramental mediation of the Church.

Taking the question a stage further, we can now ask: why is it that man tends to refer his life to a sacred reality *in just these situations?* Is there a deep reason and a special force that impels him to do so? Man's whole life is marked by a sacramental structure or 'complexity', a religious dimension, a call to the transcendent; this structure, dimension and call come forth with all their necessitating force, all their mysterious power, principally at the great, decisive moments of the life-cycle. At these moments, man finds himself needing and impelled to express his deeper reality, his basic sacramentality. In them, he finds himself at the 'threshold' through which he has to pass in order to meet the sacred, the mystery he discovers in himself and surpassing him. These are the moments of religious experience, of encounter with a totally other, unconditional, definitive and ultimate truth. On the frontiers of his life, which partly correspond to his vital transitions, man obtains a more clearsighted perception of the nearness and presence of God. If plunging deeper into his own immanence makes his own mystery transparent, this transparency calls him to transcendence in the mystery of God.[18]

All this means that when a Christian asks for a sacrament, this is not a casual gesture, but a fulfilment of a deep anthropological need—the need to express this sacred dimension of his existence, his basic situation, recognizing it, celebrating it, publicizing it, consecrating it in a religious action. This is of course part of the Christian sacrament, in that it is rooted in human-religious reality, but it is not yet the Christian specificity of the sacrament since it has no direct reference to the mystery of Christ the Saviour. Sacramental religiosity has worth as religious anthropology, but not always as Christian anthropology, even when the two are closely linked in our cultural cycle. So the Church cannot reject it as a simple deformation, but neither can it accept it as the full reality. In any case, it does not have to liberate it from this anthropologico-religious dimension (since anything truly anthropological has to be theological and vice versa), but from its residue of magic and myth, which is alienating and therefore anti-human and anti-theological.

A THEOLOGICAL EVALUATION

A theological evaluation of sacramental religiosity must set itself the task of investigating how far this religiosity includes, assumes and expresses the true content and meaning of the mystery of God, revealed and brought about in Christ, and experienced and celebrated in the Church through the sacraments.

It must be a modest attempt to show—at least in some central aspects—what degree of con-cordance or dis-cordance exists between what the subjects seek, believe and express in the sacraments and what the sacraments mean, express and offer man. This means plunging right into the controversial question of 'faith-sacrament'.

So as to avoid misunderstandings, let us establish at the outset that this is not an attempt to 'measure' the subjects' faith, nor to evaluate it in terms of its capacity for self-expression, nor to judge it according to the number of truths it knows, or religious observances it fulfils. We know their faith is simple and elemental, not 'enlightened', 'mature', or 'committed'. It works on the level of cultural Christianity, not that of the gospel ideal. So what theological criteria can be used to evaluate it?

On principle, one can say that those who are most disposed to accept the gift God offers them in the sacraments of the Church in a spirit of openness, gratitude and sincerity, have the most faith. Their acceptance supposes, at least implicitly and in general terms, that they want and believe in the bringing-about of the saving mystery of God in Christ, through the Church, at a particular point in their lives, which will be transformed and committed in a new direction after this event. Let us look at this more specifically.[19]

A sacrament means making present and *bringing about the mystery of Christ*. An attitude of sacramental faith that fails to imply reference to Christ, or contradicts it, is theologically unacceptable. Anyone who accepts God (a superior being) but does not believe in Christ (i.e., in his divinity), or vice versa, does not have faith in the God of Jesus Christ, and lacks the central and specific point of reference of sacramental faith. The God of sacramental religiosity is often a God 'with no face and no name', not historical but cosmic, belonging to myth and not the gospel, not Christian but pagan. The young in particular are prone to a 'de-divinized' God or simply 'a question-mark'.

A sacrament is also the privileged intervention of God 'here and now', *in the Church and through the Church*, as the visible Body of Christ and the People of God to whom we belong. Anyone who claims to 'believe in God' but not 'accept the Church' or belonging to it, lacks the faith God requires for celebrating the sacraments of the Church. For many of these Christians, the Church is either 'nothing', as they reject it; or it is everything, since they absolutize its mediation; or it is no more than the obligatory official place for religious rites, because they reduce it to a sort of 'ritual agency' for their moments of transition.

Sacramental faith also implies acceptance of the *proper meaning* of the sacraments as visible signs making God's intervention in the Church present in this sacramental situation. All the sacraments celebrate the same, unique mystery, but each sacrament has its theological specificity. Those who believe in God and the Church, but not in the sacraments—or in the sacrament they are celebrating—do not possess truly Christian, or authentically ecclesial, faith. If they ask for the sacraments, this is—they say—because they 'believe' in them. But *what* do they believe? Often in the rite, not in the sacrament; in the sacred reality, not in the saving Mystery of Christ; in the 'sacraments' of the life-cycle, not the sacraments of the Church.

Finally, we should remember that a sacrament is at once a *transformation*, a *liberation* and a *task*. It transforms life through the gratuitous action of God in the Spirit; it frees it from all its slaveries in the saving liberation of Christ; it commits it in all its being to act in the sense proper to the sacrament. These Christians often believe only in the more or less 'magical' effectiveness of the rite, not in the gratuitousness of the gift . . . . They are far from experiencing the sacrament as an evangelical sign of justice and freedom, as a 'confrontation' and commitment, as a transforming and renewing gift.

Of course, this rather stark contrast is generalized and somewhat idealistic (what Christian rightly experiences all these aspects?). There are many good things in sacramental religiosity: a germ of Christianity, simplicity, openness, appreciation of ritual and symbolism, trust in God, a sense of basic offering, a capacity for admiration of mystery, a non-rationalistic reasoning of faith, and an indestrüctible hope . . . . none of these should be despised. Their faith is, sometimes, no more deficient than that of some 'enlightened' Christians who always see suspicions of magic and superstition in ritual, whose celebrations are élitist, dominated by verbalism and moralism, a fruit of politics and compromise . . . But this recognition should not invalidate criticism.

Christians who practise sacramental religiosity are 'religious' Christians rather than 'believing' Catholics. Their religion is not lacking in human meaning, but it is in Christian content; it is not deficient in feeling and subjectivity, but it is in historical dimension and commitment to life. Its content has an initial impregnation with Christianity, which then needs purifying, developing, renewing, referring to experience; its sacraments have a strong cosmic-vital and religious charge, which needs to be Christianized and ecclesialized, to be brought to bear on their lives. They are, in short, 'intermediate' (half-way) Christians: [20] neither atheists nor believers, neither non-baptized, nor baptized followers. Sacramental religiosity is a fact to be taken into account, not an ideal state in which to remain.

A PASTORAL CRITIQUE

If what we have described so far amounts to a reality far removed from the 'ideal', as put forward by the Church in its historical self-understanding of an 'ought-to-be' approximating as closely as possible to the demands of the gospel, then it follows that we must look for a way out of this situation.

An initial word of warning: we should not accept any pastoral solution that starts from divisiveness or radical antagonisms (élite-mass; 'all or nothing'; evangelization or sacraments). Besides involving a denial of reality, these imply certain dangers—of division, or élitism, aggressiveness, abandonment of faith, Pharisaism—which, apart from their anti-evangelical and anti-ecclesial content, nullify any efficacity of means and exacerbate the situation they seek to remedy.

In view of the framework laid down by the Church in its reform of the sacraments, it would seem that any pastoral theory suited to 'sacramental religiosity' would, in the first place, have to be *realistic:* that is, it must understand, respect and take account of popular religiosity with all its values and riches, in a serious endeavour to improve it, without losing sight of the limits, tempo and manner appropriate to any popular pedagogical undertaking. This being so, it must start with a clear understanding of its objectives, and apply the means necessary for their attainment with consistency, while remaining continually prepared to revise them, so as to achieve a satisfactory and coherent interaction with the people instead of acting at loggerheads with them.

In the second place, it has to be *dialectical,* so that instead of opposing élite and masses, cultic religion and prophetic religion, subjective dimension and historical dimension, and soon, it works toward a synthesis, a balance of aspects, because all are equally necessary for the whole Christian and for the life of the Church. It should be perfectly clear that popular religiosity and minority religion are complementary entities in need of each other, not mutually exclusive. Neither the masses nor the élite possess a monopoly of evangelical commitment or of belonging to the Church. Rather than supposing a 'syncretism' attempting to combine opposites, if not contradictions, in a so-called synthesis, this requires concentration on the genuine aspects of the two poles of the masses-élite dialectic, not on their false aspects.

What we are undoubtedly looking for, in the third place, is an *evangelical pastoral approach,* one that purifies and de-alienates, that aims at radical conversion to sincere faith, that both values and relativizes the religious symbols and culture of the people, that helps a man to be more of a man and more of a Christian in the world. The best time (sometimes the only time) to evangelize sacramental religiosity is the time when the sacraments are sought and celebrated. Sacramental religiosity suffers not from an excess of ritual but from a lack of true sacraments; only through evangelizing the ritual will its sacraments become those of Christ and his Church.

If we are to achieve this, we need a pastoral *practice of welcome, preparation and discernment.* No, not a sort of obstacle race; it is a matter of creating the right sort of space and time for mutual understanding, meeting, quest, freedom, authenticity, prayer . . . as a preparation for the sacrament. I am well aware of the efforts and difficulties this implies—new structures, time and personnel, complications, opposition from the people; nor should we ignore the distortions it can result in—rationalism of faith, doctrinal polarization, partiality of criteria, marginalization of 'the ritual task', and so on. But I see no better way of achieving the desired objectives: a rite uninformed by faith is a rite de-formed in worship. Also, whilst discrimination is to be avoided, discernment could, I think, be used to provide different pastoral approaches and sacramental celebrations, having regard to the different situations in which people find themselves, and the differences in degree of their belonging to the Church.

And if this pastoral practice is to be effective and appear 'meaningful', there is a need to 're-think the form of the sacraments',[21] to approve new steps towards their celebration. Such might be: introduction of an interval between welcome and celebration, in all normal cases; creation of intermediate rites, or 'threshold liturgies', for those borderline, 'pre-sacramental', situations where the subjects seem to be neither 'in nor out of' the Church; universalization of a catechumenate before Confirmation in adolescence, which pre-supposes a re-arrangement of the overall initiation process in which baptism could be delayed at will and the eucharist in the adult assembly would come to be seen as the culmination of the process; promotion of popular liturgies for commemorating and renewing sacramental events—baptism in the Easter liturgy, marriage and maternity at Christmas, confirmation at Pentecost; formation of secular institutes and schools to be responsible for devising and carrying-out 'specialized' approaches to and celebration of each sacrament.

Finally, this pastoral approach can only come about and meet its requirements if it is made *with and from the people*. All that has been said, obviously and for well-known reasons, raises the question of new responsibilities and ministries in the Church and in local communities. These new ministries must be brought about if the pastoral work needed is to be done: this will really be doing pastoral work with the people. Also, if the people are not to see this pastoral work as something put upon them (as a new effort by the Church to carve out new spheres of influence for itself, perhaps), it must be seen to come from the people. That is, it must respect the rhythm of their lives and their feelings; it must sincerely propose measures, not impose them without respect; it must create rather than suppress; it must be prepared to take risks rather than seek guarantees in human terms. Even while allowing for a certain degree of creative autonomy with regard to the liturgy in forms of popular religiosity (total integration as an idea can only lead to a rejected graft),[22] this pastoral endeavour from the people needs a double movement: popularizing the liturgical (sacramental), and liturgicizing (sacramentalizing) the popular.

There has to be a 'better offer' on all levels—the form of the sacraments, the content of faith, pastoral means—as a necessary condition to combat the progressive dis-identification with the Church in its sacramental life ('if it is the same for all, who is it designed for?'). Necessary to bring those outside in, and to stop those inside from leaving.

Translated by Paul Burns

Notes

1. Popular religiosity, like religion, is first and foremost a human subject, about men, and so eminently inter-disciplinary.

2. As a help to 'situating' this field of study, here is a list of the various 'forms' of 'popular religiosity' usually distinguished: celebrations of the life cycle—birth, puberty, procreation, sickness, death = sacraments; seasonal celebrations, or celebrations of the annual cycle—spring, summer, fall and winter = the liturgical year; popular festivals—sanctuaries, pilgrimages, patron saints, processions = sacred time and space; traditional religious organizations—brotherhoods, confraternities, associations = religious communication; private devotionalism—the Sacred Heart, St Anthony, St Nicholas . . . 'favours' = individual protection and sanctification; residual forms of pre-Christian belief and degraded forms—witches, wise men, spirits, apparitions, private revelations, 'miracles' = (often) magic and manipulation of the sacred. Cf. A. L. Orensanz, *Religiosidad popular española, 1939–1965* (Madrid, 1975); F. Urbina, 'Acercamiento al tema de la religiosidad popular', in *Phase* 89 (1975), p. 340; idem., 'Reflexión pastoral sobre la religiosidad popular', in *Proyección* 96 (1975), pp. 160–68.

3. This analysis, extended to the various fields of popular religiosity, has been the subject of several studies in recent years, particularly in Latin American and Latin European spheres. Among major ones are: S. Galilea, *Analisis empírico de la religiosidad latino-americana* (Quito, 1969); Bunting, Galilea and others, *Catolicismo popular* (Quito, 1970); S. Bonnet, *A hue et è dia* (Paris, 1973); R. Pannet, *Le catholicisme populaire* (Paris, 1974); L. Maldonado, 'Religiosidad popular, Nostalgia de lo mágico', in *Cristiandad* (Madrid, 1975); SELADOC team, *Religiosidad popular* (Salamanca, 1976); R. Alvárez Gastón, *La religión del pueblo: defensa de sus valores* (Madrid, 1976). In addition, various reviews have devoted numbers to the subject: *Revista de catequesis Latino-americana, Christus, Yelda, Pastoral Misionera, Proyección, Phase, La Maison-Dieu, Concilium.*

4. I do not think it necessary for present purposes to dwell on attitudes and practices relating to each sacrament. For this, see R. Pannet, op. cit.

5. Cf. A. M. Greeley, *Religion in the Year 2000* (New York, 1969); D. Schatz (ed.), *Hat die Religion Zukunft?* (Graz & Vienna, 1971).

6. Cf. T. Luckman, 'Verfall, Fortbestand oder Verwendlung des Religiösen in der modernen Gesellschaft? in Schatz, op. cit., pp. 69–82; for the situation in Socialist countries, see K. Richter, 'Rites and symbols in industrialized cultures', in *Concilium* 122 (1977).

7. Besides the rites in their *'Prenotanda'*, the two documents that explain and insist on this need most are the Apostolic Exhortations *Marialis Cultus* (2 Feb. 1974) and *Evangelii Nuntiandi* (26 Oct. 1975).

8. Cf. D. Borobio, 'Religiosidad popular en la renovación litúrgica: Criterios para una valoración', in *Phase* 89 (1975), pp. 345–64; ibid. '¿Posreforma litúrgica en los jóvenes frente a reforma litúrgica en la iglesia?', in *Phase* 97 (1977), pp. 33–51.

9. H. Assmann, *A Practical Theology of Liberation* (London & New York, 1976); cf. L. Maldonado, 'Sugerencias preliminares para una valoración teológica de la religiosidad popular', in *Pastoral Misionera* I (1975), pp. 67–83.

10. R. Pannet, op. cit., p. 107.

11. F. Boaso, '¿Que es la religiosidad popular?', in SELADOC, op. cit., p. 116.

12. This situation poses the serious theological question of 'belonging', as has been well demonstrated in H. Bourgeois, 'Le Christianisme populaire. Un problème d'anthropologie théologique', in *La Maison-Dieu* 122 (1975), pp. 116–41.

13. J. D. Martín Velasco, 'Religiosidad popular; religiosidad popularizada y religión oficial', in *P. M.* I (1975), pp. 46–66.

14. Cf. A. Vergote, 'La réalization symbolique dans l'expression cultuelle', in *La M-D* 111 (1972), pp. 110–31; id., *Interprétation du langage religieux* (Paris, 1974); J. Cazeneuve, *Les rites et la condition humaine* (Paris, 1958).

15. Cf. R. Panikkar, *Worship and Secular Man* (London, 1973).

16. V. the theory of A. Van Gennep, in *Les rites de passage* (Paris-The Hague, 1969), in which he establishes sub-categories within the concept: 'rites de separation', 'rites de marge' and 'rites d'agrégation', esp. pp. 13–15.

17. Even recognizing an historical relativity on this point, theologically the fact that the sacraments should coincide with times of biological transition seems to me less debatable than that they should be these sacraments and not others (*v. gr.* puberty=confirmation; sickness=last rites). One would also have to ask whether the primacy in their celebration belongs to the subject or the community—in child baptism and death, others celebrate for me —, which would call the present order of receiving the Christian sacraments into question and perhaps suggest its revision.

18. The principle studies on these ideas are those of M. Eliade, R. Otto, C. Van der Loeuw, K. Rahner, J. Ratzinger, P. Tillich, R. Panikkar.

19. Cf. D. Borobio, *Matrimonio cristiano . . . ¿Para quién?* (Bilbao, 1977), pp. 93–121.

20. Cf. R. Vidales, 'Sacramentos y religiosidad popular', in SELADOC op. cit., pp. 171–87.

21. Cf. H. Denis, 'Les stratégies possibles pour la gestion de la religion populaire', in *La M-D* 122 (1975), pp. 163–93. I agree with the 'options' he notes.

22. Cf. S. Marsilli, 'Liturgia e devocioni: tra storia e teologia', in *Rivista Liturgica* 2 (1976), pp. 174–98, esp. 193–98.

David Power

The Odyssey of Man in Christ

THE PRESENT position on life-cycle rites was succinctly stated by
Klemens Richter in last year's issue of *Concilium* on *Culture, Religious
Traditions and Liturgies*.[1] Ritual serves to cope with the phases and
passages of the life-cycle, particularly with birth, adolescence, marriage and death. In traditionally Christian countries such rites became
in the course of centuries the exclusive concern of the churches. The
need was provided to a great extent through adaptations and some
distortions of the sacraments of baptism, confirmation, marriage and
anointing.[2] Even though there has been some movement to establish
civil rites and institutions to replace church rites, the situation today is
much the same.

In face of this tendency to link Christian ritual to key moments of the
life-cycle there are two pastoral issues involved, both in need of
theological reflection and pastoral discretion. The first is whether the
church community would do better to refuse ecclesial celebration of
these events to those who show little Christian faith. This has been
much debated in recent years, and the debate has served to bring
attention to the necessary faith dimension of the sacraments. The second issue is whether the special character of Christian worship which
emphasizes personal conversion, faith and *eschaton* can properly
emerge in celebrations of the life-cycle, or whether such celebration is
not more properly the province of civil institutions. It is this latter
question that is addressed in this *Concilium,* though needless to say its
discussion has some bearing on the first issue.

FAULTY SOLUTIONS

No solution to this question which is based on the sevenfold sacramental system will serve. One cannot relate the seven sacraments to moments of the life-cycle.[3] This only distorts their meaning, as appears from the history of baptism, confirmation or the anointing of the sick. As Daniel Stevick comments about the sacraments of initiation, 'it is psychologically self-defeating to try to associate one part of the initiatory unity with one stage of life, and other parts with other stages when no such staged-out meanings belong inherently to the rites themselves'.[4]

Neither can one decide that because scriptures or early tradition do not provide us with instances of liturgies for these passages of life that such may not legitimately exist. This would be to take an approach to liturgy which refutes anything that has not a direct warrant in scripture or the early church. That road prevents any serious acculturation or development of worship. In relating worship patterns to Scripture we are not confined to the rites accredited by the Scriptures. What is more important is attention to the ongoing use of its symbols and historical master images.

The celebration of the passages of the life-cycle must then be distinguished from the meaning and pastoral implications of what have come to be known as the seven sacraments. If this point were clearly accepted, there would be room to modify such practices as infant baptism, the use of confirmation as a personal ratification of baptism,[5] or the conferring of extreme unction.

The aspect of 'rites of passage' which is found in the sacraments is associated with a phase of personal conversion and with personal choice, rather than with any fixed moment in the course of a person's life. The sacraments of initiation seal a process of personal conversion whose start, duration and moment of completion are particular to every individual. Penance too is linked with passage and conversion, and while this may be provoked by many a crisis related to the time of life it is not of its nature linked with any particular crisis. The anointing of the sick is for that passage in the course of illness or old age whereby a person achieves in faith the integration of his suffering and temporality with his call to eternal life. But it has nothing particular to do with the moment of dying, nor is it necessarily found at the beginning of an illness. It is hardly necessary to emphasize the point that the change in status and interiority marked by ordination can come at any stage of a man's life.

If there are then to be rituals for the key-moments of the life-cycle they have a form and a meaning distinct from the traditional sacraments. They are rather rites to mark the occasions on which the question of personal passage symbolized in the sacraments is raised within the context of crisis moments belonging to the life-cycle as such.

THE EXAMPLE OF MARRIAGE

In fact, the only sacramental ritual which bears intrinsic reference to the life-cycle is that of marriage. For the very reason that marriage was not originally included in the sevenfold list of sacraments *as a rite,* it can serve as a good example to see what happens when moments of the life-cycle are ritualized in the Church.

It is important to bear in mind that it was originally the union between Christian spouses which was deemed to have sacramental meaning.[6] The rites of marriage were not Christian rites, but cultural customs. It was the subordination of marriage to ecclesiastical dominion that caused these rites to be modified or added to, and hence to be considered a sacrament.

It was normal that in a Christian culture the rite should be Christianized, but does that mean that today the same may hold? The Church might well return to the traditional view which finds sacramentality in the marriage union of a Christian couple and forget about a special rite whereby to celebrate its initiation. Even for its own members it could accept the validity of the civil or customary rituals, whatever they may be. The solution is a good one in as much as it leaves the regulation of all marriages to civil society. It has its flaws however if it means eliminating all celebration of marriage in church (i.e., in the Church community). Granted that it need not be a condition for valid marriage between Christians or Catholics, nor a substitution for civil rites, a rite which marks the intention 'to marry in the Lord' and acquire the Church's blessing seems appropriate. In a secularized culture, and even while accepting the values of the secular project, people need a way to express and appropriate the Christian vision of marriage. The more people are doubtful about the adequacy of society's approach to marriage, the more this seems necessary. The Church's, or the couple's, sense of being different,[7] of having a singular approach to marriage and the sexual order, merits the experience and the symbolic expression of the liturgy.

A mere repetition, however, of ancient rituals is not what is expedient. The Churches need to engage in an imaginative reworking of the symbols, which would include an incorporation of the valid insights peculiar to the evolution of cultures. There is an anthropological basis to Christian symbolism in the marriage union itself, which is experienced as a 'limit situation' in human life, involving as it does a close intimacy between two persons and an option about their future existence. It is on the seeking of partnership between two persons that the symbolism of Christ's union with his Church is based, and as in all cases of symbolism the first meaning is necessary to the second. Yet the original, personal, meaning does not simply lead into the second. An act of faith is required, a readiness to trust the partnership to God and to take the model of Christian *agapé* whereon to stake the future. Hence, even though the sacramentality of the union is not to be confused with the rite, and a sacramental marriage in faith can exist without it, a rite which expresses the Christian symbolism of marriage seems appropriate to its inception.

This example of marriage is a good paradigm on which to base an understanding of all life-cycle rituals. Generally, cultures have rites for the moments of birth and death, and often also for adolescence. In a Christian civilization they were subjected in one way or another to ecclesiastical dominion. In a secular culture (and with due modification the same thing would hold true for a non-Christian religious culture) the rites and institutions appropriate to these moments could well be set free from this monopoly, even in the case of the Churches' own members. The question however remains whether some distinctively Christian way of marking them would not be appropriate. There are grave and perilous human questions involved in each such passage, questions touching the individual and his communities, but there is also a distinctive way of facing them in the faith and hope of Christ.[8] In each case, the human meaning is fundamental, but on the first meaning a second signification is based when it is incorporated into the Lord.

CHRISTIAN MEANING AND SYMBOL

Antecedent to the question of a specific Christian rite for the moments of passage there is the question of how these moments are perceived in a vision of faith. Three steps need to be worked out as an answer to this. The first is to thoroughly enter into the current cultural experience. In the Western world, this means to take the secular culture seriously. We need to know its crises and its fears, its values and its valid insights into the human condition, as well as the intimations of the sacred inherent to its enterprise.[9] This step will raise some serious questions about the ways in which our Christian past has viewed questions of birth, marriage and death. Hence the second step will be a study of Christian symbols and their usage which will investigate the reasons for some of our past Christian interpretations, as well as the possibility of a more constructive one. The third and final step would be to use these symbols in such a way as to integrate the secular (or other cultural) experience. This implies a speaking in Christian symbols which so interprets the secular experience as to include it in the mystery of Christ, make it an integral part of the history wherein the God of Abraham, Isaac and Jacob pursues his quest for a holy alliance with man. The secular project itself might be best saved within this horizon.[10]

THE SECULAR EXPERIENCE OF PASSAGES

All the moments of the life-cycle are deeply affected by the influence of a secular culture. A brief glance at each one will have to suffice here.

It is the changing relationship between the sexes which is at the core of the contemporary experience of marriage, and which raises questions about the way that it has been understood for so long in the Christian Churches. It is an area where feelings are high, where no clear solutions are to be found, where the whole structure of society is at stake. There is no more supposedly 'God-given' pattern to be obediently followed, yet the enterprise is in need of a model to direct its explorations.

In the case of birth, not all questions about the communication of life are so easily solved as they were by a natural law ethic. New values and new desires have arisen, not unrelated to the man-woman relationship, and they are regulated by an evaluation of life other than that based on obedience to the physical laws of generativity. Added to this dilemma, there is the threat to nascent life which seems inherent to our world because of oppression, fear, social and political structures.

Today's adolescent is the quintessence of the lost individual, with no heroes, no standard values, no society in which to believe, yet exploited by the economic forces of the very order against which he rebels. Those endowed with genius and with spirit sometimes try to escape from the order and try out new patterns of living and human intercourse. These are their contributions to the life-force, which may drift on the wind or may perhaps be both unleashed and harnassed to greater purpose.

In face of death, we are certainly given pause by Ernest Becker's claim that much of our present posturing is dictated by the innate reluctance to accept death's inevitability. This says much about the drives which are the undercurrent of development.[11] Yet the death of secular man is not without its force and dignity, as evidenced in Becker's own case.

It is clear that much of what was found in the Christian stance on these issues neither meets the fears nor takes in the values of the secular vision. The inferiority of women in the Churches, sanctioned by marriage rites, the understanding that purification is cleansing from sexual experience, or that a person must be baptized at birth because born an enemy of God, are poor ways to live full lives in the hope of the coming of the kingdom. Is some recovery of the symbolism behind such interpretations possible, a recovery which would give constructive hope to present searchings?

CHRISTIAN SYMBOLS OF PASSAGES

We shall first of all follow up the example of marriage and take the sexual symbolism as it is put to use in the *velatio nuptialis* of the *Verona Sacramentary*.[12] As used in that source, the imagery clearly postulates the subjection of woman to man, and the marriage is wholly directed to the purpose of procreation. If one relates it to the blessing of virgins in the same sacramentary,[13] one can see that there is no absence of distrust and misgiving about the body's role in God's plan. The prayers witness to the fact that a need for redemption is clearly felt. In other words, inherent to the apparent experience of marriage and sexuality was the sense that something had gone wrong and needed to be set aright. It is in an appeal to the original order of creation and its redemption in Christ that salvation is sought. While we draw back now from the use to which this appeal is put, we can nonetheless ask whether in the symbolism itself there is not a meaning which is still viable.

The symbolism is based on Gen 1:27 and on the redemption of this primitive order through Jesus Christ. This does not have to be interpreted in the way it is used in the source quoted. In fact, when we complete Gen 1:27 with Gal 3:28 and Matt 19:4–5, we can see that the order signified in these symbols, and therefore that which is to be restored, is the completeness of human nature as male and female, and the equal partnership in love of woman and man.[14]

Some residual fear of the body and guilt about sex remain with us today, but the greatest difficulties to be met in entering marriage now come from the misconstruction of the woman-man relationship and the need to set it aright. The Christian symbolism we have referred to is therefore very relevant to the current situation, and its eschatological vision of an order restored in Christ can fortify persons entering into the marriage union.

Whereas today we are moving away from a privatization of life and from a stoic concept of natural law, there are many private and public issues which surround the birth of a new human person. In past centuries, the symbols which affected birth centred around the understanding that infant baptism was a cleansing from original stain and that the blessing of a mother after childbirth was a purification necessarily consequent on certain bodily functionings. This use of symbols was in keeping with the privatization of religion and with the sense of obedience to an imposed order. Again, however, when we probe the symbolism we find that it has a basis which allows a more open and constructive interpretation.

Purification is not a matter of bodily cleanliness, nor necessarily a connotation of wrong-doing or inferiority. The pure and the impure refer to place in a given order.[15] There are encounters with the sacred which escape the control of order, which involve hazards and risks for the person and for society. Hence such encounters may involve a person in 'impurity', necessitating that one be set for a while on the boundaries of the community, until such time as reintegration (purification) may be deemed expedient. This re-entry is ritualized, so that the power of the sacred may be taken into the community, while yet being made to fit into the established order. A mother and her new-born child are a sacred being. They represent the mystery of life at its source and so they are outside the order of clear social control. Hence they are put on the periphery, for as long as the aura of the sacred surrounds them. Purification is a re-entry of mother and child into the human community, as new life, new vigour, new revelation.

Similar considerations can be offered on the myth and symbol of original sin. Far from being the private symbol embodied in a theory of sinful inheritance and personal stain, it is a social and communitarian symbol, reflecting solidarity in sin and death. The awareness of this solidarity can be particularly poignant at the moment of the birth of a child, but it can also be countered by faith in solidarity in Christ. In fact, the primary symbolism in the Christian economy is always that of Christ, that of redemption, that of messianic hope. In that sense, the symbolism of original sin, or sin in the first Adam, is secondary and ought to be used as such.

Symbols which express corporate evil and corporate hope seem appropriate to the issues with which society is often faced today and which emerge in a particular way when questions of life and birth are at stake. Furthermore, the symbols which we have indicated as traditional are not necessarily restricted to infant baptism, but could be used in some other form of rite.

In Christian tradition, there is no particular symbol or ceremony associated with the transition to adult maturity. At the same time, maturation in Christian faith, or initiation understood as personal conversion and personal choice, is necessary at this stage of life. It is a phase of life in which to acquire a personal identity and a sense of belonging in adult society. It is a moment when a person is faced with the choice to adopt or reject the meanings and symbols of his culture. This is an experience which is gravely traumatic today when society and culture are disintegrating. One may then well ask whether anything in the christian story could fortify a youth in this life-passage.[16]

RITUAL

To have said that Christian symbols may serve to interpret the life experience in a secular culture is not yet to have settled for any particular form of ritual. Certain forms of passage rites create problems for the secular project and for Christian worship alike, and it is well to be aware of this. These belong in a peculiar way to a cosmocentric vision of the world, and seek to absorb human life into the flow of the seasons and the movements of the cosmic bodies. This includes a sense of time which is based on archaic myths, involving a repetition of the 'timeless' and a closure on future possibilities.

The secular project, on the contrary, is anthropocentric, not cosmocentric. Its great moments are not those which cause man to merge into the movements of the cosmos, and it is alien to anything which treats birth, sexual experience, or even death, in this way. Its own moments are those of human achievement, of the unbinding of Prometheus. Secular man needs the symbols which give meaning to his own vigour and personal enterprise, for he wishes to relate himself to the given of the world and to time itself on this basis.

Cosmic ritual and mythic repetition also go counter to the core meaning of Christian worship, with its proclamation of the abiding *hodie* of salvation and of the free gift of God's love and grace. This makes nonsense of enslavement to rhythm or circular repetition. The memorial of Christian worship is a moment in history, which takes its meaning and its hope from the resurrection of Christ. It is not the remembering of a repetitious drama. It is the redemption of time and its passing events, through their integration into salvation in the memory of Christ.

An authentic Christian symbolism frees the life-phases or passages from enslavement to cosmic rhythms. They are instead turned into moments of revelation, of the event of God's salvation, of the freeing of the Spirit. The time is endowed with more freedom and hope than it is in its own power to warrant, because it is redeemed in Christ and made a moment of the giving of the Spirit who frees and recreates. In other words, something new is given to the phases of the human life-cycle because of Christ and the gift of his Spirit. William Lynch expresses this admirably when he writes: 'The phases of the life of Christ are the mysteries of Christ. But it is the time and phases, the odyssey of man, which he re-explores'.[17]

RITUAL AND IMAGINATION

The place of imagining is crucial in rituals of the life-cycle if we are to avoid the danger of conforming to repetitive patterns. It is when Christianity fails in imagination where the life of the body is concerned that this is subjected, in God's name, to the repetitive physical patterns of the body cycle of sexual reproduction, birth, sexual awakening, and death.

Liturgy which is not of the body is untrue. The natural infrastructure is present in Christian worship, both the sense of bodily functionings and the awareness of the cosmos. But it is the work of Christian imagination, in the memory of Christ, to remind us that through the presence of God in man's history man can be free and creative. He can transcend, even while integrating, his partnership with the earth and with the heavens.

Such transcendence does not mean that we deny the experience of nothingness which is so sharp in the moments of human passage. It means rather getting in touch with the permanent which can emerge just as sharply in these moments. This permanent is built not on submission to the tragic inability to overcome our bodily finitude, nor on man's own achievement, but on the capacity for God which is filled with God's own love.

This is a very freeing image, both for Christian hope and for the secular project of a more human earth. It makes us aware that life's possibilities are not determined by the physical boundaries of birth, reproduction and mortality. Hence there is no law which tells us that faith in God imposes a blind obedience to these boundaries. On the other hand, it is not technical success in the manipulation of these boundaries which holds out future promise. By focusing on the memory of Jesus Christ the Christian imagination offers other ways to explore the meaning of these moments. It suggests to us that it is because in these moments we are put in touch with the weakest and most vulnerable part of ourselves that they are so rich in the promise of life. Remembering the way in which Christ encountered human weakness, his own and that of others, reveals to us that in this very vulnerability is their power. He neither denied nor manipulated weakness. He 'passed through it'. By this memory we are called to an awareness of our own simultaneous temporality and immortality. For anybody who arrives at that centre of consciousness, the present is full of possibilities. The trials, the questions, the problems and the suffering are not dismissed, but they can be faced in a new way.

This is vital to the question of Christian rites for the moments of the life-cycle. How we deal with new life and its reproduction, with sexuality, with death is of immense importance for the future. Every society has its projects and its hopes for the future, and often enough they centre around these realities. Christians can in many cases concur with the symbols and institutions in which these hopes are expressed, or at least they are ready to discuss them in open forum. At the same time, through faith in Christ they see that all future possibility depends on the *hodie* of God and man in covenant. This can be of great consequence for a Christian's contribution to the secular, or any other cultural, project.

LIFE-CYCLE RITUAL AND SACRAMENTS

At the outset of this article, it was said that the traditional seven sacraments may not be used to answer the needs of life-cycle ritual. At the same time, it would be wrong to give the impression that there are two ritual systems possible in the church, the one that of the sacraments and the other that of the life-cycle. The latter have to be related to the former, and the nature of the relation lies in the *call* to personal conversion experienced at moments of the life-cycle and expressed in terms of christian belief in these rites.

An answer to the meaning of human life can be given at birth through the Christian symbols of the holy and of redemption. This necessarily raises the question of initiation in the faith and of membership of the Christian community. Pastors and theologians today often suggest that birth or infancy is not the appropriate moment for baptism. Instead they indicate the possibility of a rite of welcome and inscription, which envisages the eventual initiation and personal faith of the child. This could well be associated with the Christian symbols of birth, important to the parents in commencing the education of their child in the Christian faith, and in the fulness of the life which is God's gift. The moment of personal initiation would then be decided in later years by the child's own personal choice, while at the same time it is prepared within the community from his birth.

The question of conversion and Christian belonging is raised for the growing person at many critical moments, and chiefly in adolescence. Any rites related to growth serve to raise the issue of personal initiation, and can be steps whereby through a personal integration of the factors involved in the growth process a young person moves towards faith in Christ.

In the case of marriage, it seems a great mistake to make a valid (and genuinely human) marriage and sacramental marriage coincide in time. The rites occurring at the beginning of marriage call for a personal evaluation of its meaning, but they may not in effect signify as yet a deep personal faith on the part of the marriage partners. The marriage becomes truly sacramental when it can be said that through personal faith it is lived by both partners in the Lord. It may be hard to express an exact moment at which this is the case, but it is more in the eucharist than in a marriage ritual postulated at the inception of marriage that the sealing in faith often takes place. If the Church were to maintain a marriage sacrament (i.e., rite) truly signifying the personal choice to be married in Christ, this would have to be dissociated from the beginning of marriage and allowed for at a moment chosen in faith by the partners, within the compass of their experience of marriage. A marriage ceremony at the inception of marriage is more in the nature of a call to faith and to live marriage in faith.

CONCLUSION

I began this article by recalling the place of life-cycle rites in diverse cultures, and the position of these rites in traditionally Christian countries. I then said that the problems which this raises today cannot be answered by an appeal to the sevenfold sacramental system, nor on the direct evidence of the scriptures. Through the example of marriage, I then showed how human meaning can be integrated into the Christian. After a brief word about the current secular experience of passages, I indicated that the traditional Christian symbols relevant to these moments can include the secular values, while respecting their own intrinsic validity. The next step was to examine the implications of ritual, and to suggest that the ritual used in moments of passage when celebrated in the memory of Christ can be an open and transcending experience, revealing the *hodie* of salvation and the presence of God's Spirit in man.

We may then conclude that Christian rituals might well express the meaning of life-cycle events, without suppressing either authentic secularity or authentic Christian faith. On the other hand, the prevalent use of some of the sacraments does not constitute an adequate ritual, but rather does disservice to these sacraments. A recovery of the meaning of some traditional symbols may result in attempts to bring fresh understanding to explorations in ritual. What would be the end result of this is hard to tell. We can agree with L. Bertsch, as he is quoted in the article by K. Richter, already mentioned: 'Neither the repetition of doctrinal formulas nor the rational planification of new rites will bring the solution, but only the road which leads towards a faith ever on the increase, and on the basis of which new ritual forms of comportment and ecclesial life can be found'.[18]

Notes

1. Klemens Richter, in *Concilium* (February, 1977).

2. On this process for the sacraments of initiation, cf. Nathan D. Mitchell, 'Dissolution of the Rite of Christian Initiation', Murphy Center for Liturgical Research (ed.), *Made, Not Born* (Notre Dame, 1976), pp. 50–82.

3. Aquinas's synthesis, *S. Th.* III, q. 65, art. 1, is based on an analogy with the natural life-cycle, but does not relate the sacraments to moments of the life-cycle.

4. Daniel B. Stevick, 'Christian Initiation; Post-Reformation to the Present Era', in *Made, Not Born*, p. 116.

5. Whether at the age of five or fifteen, there is little justification for presenting confirmation as a personal ratification of one's earlier baptism. Scriptural and liturgical evidence show that the two sacraments complement one another in what is signified, so that any separation goes counter to their internal meaning.

6. Cf. L.-M. Chauvet, 'Le mariage, un sacrement pas comme les autres', *La Maison-Dieu*, 127 (1976) 3, pp. 64–105.

7. Cf. Stevick, art. cit., p. 114; 'Today Christian culture is not a close, tangible reality, which supports and interprets liturgy . . . The drift of modern, secularized culture will not carry anyone to Christ, but rather in the opposite direction. The believing community, like its crucified Lord, finds itself "outside the gate" . . .'

8. The question is whether I am prepared to 'make a wager' that the Christian symbols can interpret man's being in the world, as experienced in these moments.

9. Cf. L. Gilkey, *Naming the Whirlwind; The Renewal of God-Language* (Indianapolis, 1967), pp. 305–414.

10. Cf. W. Lynch, *Christ and Prometheus; A New Image of the Secular* (Notre Dame, 1972), pp. 123–42.

11. E. Becker, *The Denial of Death* (New York & London, 1973).

12. L. C. Mohlberg (ed.), *Sacramentarium Veronense* (Rome, 1956), n. 1110.

13. Ibid., n. 1104.

14. Cf. Paul K. Jewett, *Man as Male and Female. A Study in Sexual Relationships from a Theological Point of View* (Grand Rapids, 1975).

15. Cf. Mary Douglas, *Purity and Danger* (London, 1966).

16. On death, see the article in this issue by P. Rouillard.

17. Lynch, op. cit., p. 72.

18. Richter, art. cit., pp. 112–13.

PART IV

Bulletin on Confirmation

Günter Biemer

Controversy on the Age of Confirmation as a Typical Example of Conflict between the Criteria of Theology and the Demands of Pastoral Practice

THE DISPUTE concerning the age of confirmation continues. A recent dissertation on confirmation, incorporating a comprehensive survey of the sources from the dogmatic point of view, emphasizes that in sacramental-dogmatic terms infant baptism is a 'deficient form of baptism, a borderline version of the classical model of baptism', and that this deficiency must be made up by receiving the sacrament of confirmation.[1] Apart from this dogmatic aspect, the decisive criteria for the establishment of the age at which confirmation is to be received should be pedagogical and anthropological. 'It is, so to speak, a question of expediency, a question as to the age at which the confirmation of baptism can be demanded and when it should best take place. Hence the matter is basically of an emotional and psychological nature'.[2]

This is the case if we see confirmation as the re-affirmation of baptism. If, however, we take into account the numerous theological functions and purposes presented in dogmatic writings about the sacrament of confirmation,[3] we then see that the controversy about the age of confirmation cannot be so easily resolved. This is due to three elements of uncertainty:

(a) the insufficiently precise theological definition of the nature of confirmation;

(b) the overall impossibility of establishing any one specific age at which the psychological and sociological prerequisites for confirmation are met;

(c) the relative situation arising from the correlation between theological and pedagogical-anthropological criteria.

It is this problem of relativity that has contributed to the insolubility of the controversy because it is underestimated by systematic theologians as well as by practical theologians and ecclesiastical practitioners, as this article aims to demonstrate.

THE CONTROVERSIAL THEOLOGICAL CONCEPTIONS OF CONFIRMATION AND THEIR PRACTICAL EFFECTS

1. Among the numerous approaches adopted both today and in the past the first alternative that presents itself is a more emphatically *dogmatico-ecclesiological* conception, concerned first and foremost with the sacramental link with initiation and hence the maintenance of the sequence baptism-confirmation-eucharist. Those in support of this approach refer to the historical origin of sacramental initiation and to the position and function of confirmation in this connection, and thus argue in favour of confirmation being administered as soon as possible after infant baptism; for since confirmation is linked to baptism in the process of initiation it should definitely be received before the eucharist. The most consistent form of this concept of the 'fundamental unity of the stages of initiation' must be the direct application of the theological theory to pastoral practice. This approach is practised in the infant confirmation found in the Eastern church as well as in the Ibero-American cultural sphere,[4] and is also postulated by theologians in the western Church.[5]

The *Codex Iuris Canonici* favours a later confirmation at the *age of discrimination* although maintaining the postulated sequence of the initiation sacraments.[6] Following a centuries-old tradition confirmation is not to be administered until the age of reason is reached. This *postponement model* is also based on objective ecclesiological grounds, namely the structural legality of the process of enrolment into the Church.[7]

Hans Küng is currently attempting to co-ordinate objective-theological and subjective-anthropomorphic aspects within the scope of this postponement model, in that he stipulates that the purpose of confirmation is to develop, affirm and complete (infant) baptism which it must therefore follow.[8] 'From a phenomenological point of view confirmation signifies the point—in what is naturally a long and complex development—when the child, having been baptized at the request of its believing parents publicly confirms its baptism—following a basic catechism appropriate to its age—and professes its faith before the community of the faithful. By means of a special ritual it is recognized and accepted as a full member of the community of the church and admitted to the celebration of the eucharist. Confirmation and first communion would take place in the same celebration'.[9] For the child of about eight, this 'profession of faith' implies 'an open affirmation and a responsible, publicly acknowledged decision of the young person to live his life according to the Gospel of Jesus Christ. Baptism, in the first instance only passively received by the child, now becomes fully effective through the active involvement of grace engendered by the young person's faith, profession and action'.[10]

2. Advocates of the basically *pastoral-anthropomorphic* conception of the sacraments maintain that adequate personal involvement in the sacrament of confirmation will lead to the formation of an active and responsible Church community. For this reason they propose that the age of confirmation be fixed at the earliest between the ages of twelve and sixteen. Hence the General Synod of Bishops in the Federal Republic of Germany recommends the age of twelve, with the justification: 'At that age the child is already capable of grasping much of the significance of confirmation and can thus meaningfully make a request to receive this sacrament. He is beginning to emerge from the world of childhood and the childish acceptance of faith and takes his first steps towards an independent faith. In his own way he can and must by this stage become a witness to Christ. He is able to accept and pursue the responsibility of fulfilling the most important dogma of all, to love God and one's neighbour'.[11]

At the Second Catechetical Congress held in Munich in 1928 it was proposed that the sacrament of confirmation should be administered at the age of *fifteen*.[12] This was based on the anthropological pre-requisite of the 'best disposition' for the reception of the sacrament and the ability to 'commit oneself' to the Gospel.

The extension of this line of argument, pursued significantly above all by religious educators [13] leads one to the argument propounded by Exeler: 'Infant baptism can give explicit expression to God's love and the social context of faith, but it does not include the unique act of faith on the part of the individual. It is precisely this very personal affirmation of the individual to God's coming towards us in the person of Jesus, the decisive acceptance of the community of the Church and hence the affirmation of this Church's involvement on the part of individuals, social groups and society as a whole that would find expression—as a prophetic sign also—if confirmation were only to be administered to young adults, in other words from about the age of eighteen onwards'.[14]

A series of official statements made by church teachers may be interpreted as 'open declarations' which at least do not deviate from the age recommendations made in this section.[15]

3. An anthropologically orientated theology, while maintaining a strictly theo-centrist position, nevertheless aims to link the effects of God's salvation with the history of mankind and the life of the individual. It therefore sees the sacrament of confirmation as connected with man's fundamental or existential situation: 'In the sacraments a decisive and fundamental human situation is manifest about which the significant and powerful message of the salvation of God through Jesus Christ is spoken. In this way salvation through Jesus Christ reveals itself in the human sphere by means of words and signs. The sacraments are therefore the word of salvation introduced into a fundamental human situation in the form of a symbolic ecclesiastical act (cf. *Liturgiekonstitution*, 60)'.[16]

The consequences for a corresponding practice of confirmation to be drawn from this link between anthropology and theology are as yet only in the initial stages of development.[17]

THE NATURE OF THE CONFLICT

Leaving aside the last-mentioned conception, we are confronted by two main lines of argument. Advocates of dogmatic and liturgical theology with their systematic reflections on the effects of God's salvation are concerned primarily with the *pretext of salvation* and would like to impose greater temporal unity on the sacramental initiation of children despite the separate administration of the sacraments. They therefore subordinate the human participation in faith and sacrament to their systematically argued structure. Advocates of practical theology, with their emphasis on pastoral-anthropological aspects, are primarily concerned to ensure the *human participation* and try to use the actual separation of the initiation sacraments as a process of enrolment into the Church; the act of faith, which in infant baptism is limited by the substitution necessary, should be completed and perfected by confirmation.

These two positions cannot, however, be resolved into a compromise. Rather, they postulate a pastoral-theological principle of mediation, as has already been attempted for example by Arnold with his human-divine principle of the pastoral.[18] The *'irreconcilability'* of the two positions can be deduced from the fact that for one party confirmation signifies the gift of the spirit (*character indelebilis*) as a result of which it does not seem important 'when we receive this sacrament of our spiritual majority and to what extent we have understood its meaning. It is far more important that having received confirmation we should at some point in our life finally become aware of what in fact took place then and what we personally, subjectively have to fulfil'.[19] In this way the confirmand's pastoral awareness of himself as a human being is only treated with relative seriousness: that is, in relation to future personal development. This gives rise to the question posed by advocates of pastoral theory and practice; namely, at what point should the person baptized as an infant fulfil the affirmation of the Gospel lacking in his infant baptism and essential to the process of initiation?

One can assume that all theologians and practitioners who advocate the separate administration of confirmation (following infant baptism) are hoping that the issue of the appropriate age will be resolved by the discipline relating to juvenile experience and behaviour, namely educational psychology or sociology. At this point Hans Küng's argument comes into force. Can one seriously uphold the confirmation of eight-year-olds if it can be proved psychologically and sociologically that children of that age cannot fulfil the unequivocal anthropological conditions for the *opus operantis* of the sacrament of confirmation which he formulates as 'a freely affirmative, responsible, publicly declared decision on the part of the young person to live his life according to the Gospel of Jesus Christ?' [20]

How seriously are young people regarded as real individuals in (systematic) theology, which is how they are known to community leaders? And how seriously are the results of the empirical human sciences taken by practical and systematic theology? Given that the proposed anthropological pre-requisites for the reception of confirmation could be proved to exist only between the ages of ten and fourteen or even later, would the dogmatic theologians and liturgical theorists then be prepared to alter the sequence of the initiation sacraments? Furthermore, would they agree that what is happening is not so much an initiation (which by definition takes place at once) as a lengthy process of socialization requiring years to complete? This is the potentially problematic issue arising from this context. The early Christian initiation Easter eve can truly be described as an initiation; but when applied to the structure of enrolment in the Church, as currently practised in the case of children and young people, this term is very questionable.

PSYCHOLOGICAL EXPLANATION OF THE DEVELOPMENT
OF PERSONALITY

Religious feeling or religious behaviour is. a highly complex psychological phenomenon about which very little research has as yet been carried out. The traditional psychological theory that man has an inherent disposition towards religion has undergone some modification, and it is now held that the possible development of religious feeling is to be found in the structures of the development of personality. The theory of predisposition has made us firmly aware of the distinction between the childish phase of religious feeling and puberty, when religious feeling first becomes a personal problem owing to the intensified cognitive need to find ultimate links between the individual existence and the universe.[21]

Religious development is based to a certain extent on the *maturation* of those psychological tendencies essential to the structure of the personality and likewise crucial to the religious experience. But it is also based on *processes of learning* which by means of confrontation with religious behaviour lead to decisive experiences (learning by imitation, identification with persons close to the child who practise their religion). The phenomenon of psychic structure formation is decisive in this respect. By this we mean the individual's ability to relate functions and experiences gained and to adapt them to his own needs and decisions. In using subsidiary learning [22] to work out the ultimate meaning of himself and the world the adolescent is indicating his *intentional effort* to find an all-embracing meaningful context. 'The intentional alteration of behaviour is of fundamental importance to religious development, in that it enables religious codes of behaviour acquired or adapted by the individual to be shaped into a personal religious decision and significance. Without this intentional behaviour the individual . . . is only superficially affected'.[23] The sociology of knowledge thus differentiates between man as the product of his social environment to the extent that he becomes familiar with the institutional as well as the 'religious' programme of society, identifies with them and his simultaneous rôle as co-producer: the individual 'absorbs the social world, its institutions, rôles and identities not in a passive way, but rather actively adapts them to himself and his needs'.[24]

It is in this context of active self-determination, i.e., intentional shaping of behaviour, that the psychology of cognition speaks of the integration and adaptation of previously acquired experiences (in the religious sphere, too). The development of religious feeling is to be seen in connection with this process of personalization. For without intentional and hence personal efforts to attach meaning to the world the adolescent would remain on the level of adapted and hence not independent religious behaviour.[25]

Given this approach to the development of religious or pious life and behaviour, one can see that modern developmental psychology regards the decline of orthodox attitudes at the onset of puberty as a sign of increased religious activity. For it establishes that from the age of twelve or thirteen the adolescent no longer absorbs given religious habits but tends more and more to reflect about the meaning of his own existence. In this context Oerter points out, along the same lines as D. and S. Elkind, that twelve to sixteen years is the 'earliest age for religious experiences of conversion'.[26]

With regard to the development from heteronomous to autonomous *morality* the distinction must be made between imitative moral behaviour and independent moral conceptions, as pointed out by Hurlock, whereby the latter only take shape in the course of maturation. According to Kohlberg's experimental schema of moral development, there is a marked increase in moral judgment based on personally accepted principles and personal principles of conscience from the age of thirteen onwards.[27] We should also take account of Nickel's opinion that because of the considerable overlapping of the different moral types proposed by Kohlberg it would not be possible to distinguish any specific phases of development on the basis of age,[28] but one should not draw the false conclusion that pre-moral, i.e., conventional moral judgment or behaviour vanishes on reaching adulthood. Far more decisive for religious development or moral judgment is the tendency towards independence or autonomy, beginning at the age of thirteen and increasing to the age of sixteen, as demonstrated by the above-mentioned authors.

At all events a range of typical experiences and behaviour can be ascribed to young people during and after puberty which may be summarized as follows. The transformation of the super-ego into the image of self; the experimental realization of the image of self; the growth of the instinct to extend oneself in the temporal perspective; behavioural conflict in the process of liberating the self; the tendency to autonomous moral behaviour; socialization according to one's own direction.

In comparison to the contours of the personalization process in youth, the forms of experience and behaviour found in children are destined to be replaced. The extension of the ego which constitutes (W. G. Alport) the pre-requisite for the development of the child's image of itself also forms the basis of the first self-orientated confrontation with the image of God 'so long as the image of God recognizes the limitations of the self and allows these to be accepted in trust'.[29] Six- to seven-year-olds see God as the planner of the sun, moon, stars and animals and eight- to nine-year-olds as the almighty, all-knowing creator and loving Father, in which anthropomorphic conceptions predominate.[30] Religious feeling is strongly dependent on the behaviour of the adults with whom the child identifies and in particular on the consistency of their behaviour. The participation of the self in the (religious) process of learning has begun but has not reached autonomy. As regards the child's development of conscience, in his seventh year his pragmatic orientation towards punishment and obedience takes a further step forward (the pre-moral level: Kohlberg), even before authoritarian morality under which the child (as also the juvenile and the adult) behaves in conformity with the norms for opportune reasons.

The child's typical range of behaviour consists in: the participation in the norms and rôles of society through identification; the development of the earliest forms of self-identity; heteronomous morality based on familiarization; a considerable ability to trust and to adopt models or value concepts.

THESES

1. The *mutual concern* of all who advocate or demand that confirmation be administered at a separate time to baptism is based on the idea that the person receiving the sacrament of confirmation should be able to *profess his faith personally,* in contrast to the situation in infant baptism. For this reason none of them advocates a time before the child has reached the age of reason (from about seven onwards).

2. What is in dispute is the *degree of independence* which the child should have acquired towards his faith before receiving the sacrament of confirmation:

—Faith arising out of the childish forms of self-identity and participation in the faith of adults with whom the child identifies, based on a rudimentary knowledge of the catechism and an ambivalent conscience built up from familiarization.[31]

—Faith arising out of a self-identity in the process of freeing itself from identification with influential adults, establishing a relationship with its own contemporaries and intentionally seeking after meaning; leading to confrontation with concepts of values and norms, capable of adapting catechetics to its own existential situation, and experimenting in living according to a pre-critical conscience based on responsibility.

—Faith arising from an independent concept of self and a personal belief in the Gospel of Jesus Christ, following the confrontation with world-orientated alternatives and able to strive towards existential fulfilment in career and marriage with the help of a self-critical conscience based on responsibility.

3. However the age for confirmation is fixed, *socialization of faith and reception of the sacrament of confirmation* must stand in a *firm relation* to each other by means of a catechetical concept of the community of the Church. Hence confirmands whose level of faith is that of participation with persons with whom they identify (*a*) require continued religious education after confirmation (like that after infant baptism). Confirmands whose faith is on the level of a self-identity in the process of freeing itself (*b*) must have undergone a corresponding reli-

gious socialization already and require a continuous supply of opportunities (for example, Church youth work). Confirmands who have reached the level of a faith based on an independent concept of self (c) must assume personal responsibility for the socialization of their faith; by means of the sacrament of confirmation they are incorporated in the adult community.

4. We might of course subscribe to the hypothesis put forward by J. S. Bruner: 'Every child at any stage in its development can successfully be taught anything in an intellectually honest form'. But one should bear in mind that this kind of imposition of knowledge with the aid of the psychology of learning inevitably makes it necessary to simplify a great deal, especially with regard to complex objects. In the case of teaching the faith one must investigate the danger of this leading to the over-simplification and belittling of things. This danger in turn leads to an *ideological interpretation* when psychological facts are made into norms for dogmatic reasons and thereby falsified, as for example is the case if one ascribes primarily autonomous avowals of faith to an eight-year-old that are still mainly determined by heteronomous (participatory) faith, as is the case with an independent public profession of faith before the community.

5. Anyone who sees confirmation from the dogmatic point of view as the completion and fulfilment of baptism, as the renewal of the power of the Holy Spirit already manifest in baptism and as a sacramental step towards enrolment in the Church, is confronted with the following *alternative,* given the anthropological development of man. Either we must forgo an adequate human understanding of the sacrament at the time of receiving it and seek this instead in the subsequent course of religious education and the development of conscience (which is also done in the case of infant baptism), or we must wait for that phase in a child's development, at the very earliest between the ages of twelve and fourteen, when an adolescent, motivated by the search for the meaning of the world, is capable of discussing spiritual matters.

6. In comparing confirmation and first communion we should take account of the different nature of the two sacraments. The eucharist is a continuous sacrament accompanying man throughout his life and can therefore be received in a participative way right from the start (i.e., sharing in the faith of influential adults). The Christian experiences the eucharistic encounter afresh at all stages of his life.[32] Confirmation, on the other hand, is only received once. Even if the *character indelibilis* it bestows is guaranteed to revive at a later date, there nevertheless remains the question as to whether it should not be administered at that point in a child's development when the optimal analogy exists between anthropologico-psychological aspects and the theological significance of the sacrament.

Notes

1. J. Amougou-Atangana, *Ein Sakrament des Geistempfangs? Zum Verhältnis von Taufe und Firmung* (Freidburg-Basle-Vienna, 1974), p. 301.

2. Ibid., p. 300.

3. Ibid., parts I and II; cf. G. Biemer, *Firmung. Theologie und Praxis* (Würzburg, 1973), pp. 35–45.

4. Cf. the comment by J. A. Jungmann, 'Einleitung und Kommentar zur Konstitution über die heilige Liturgie in Das Zweite Vatikanishe Konzil', I, in *Lexikon für Theologie und Kirche* (Freiburg-Basle-Vienna, 1966, pp. 10–110; p. 68.

5. Cf. E. J. Lengeling, 'Die Einheit der dreigestuften Initiation', *Diakonia*, 4 (1973), pp. 46–49. The stark contrast between the confirmation of infants and a 'spirituality infused with faith in the power of the spirit' is raised by L. Ligier with reference to the Eastern Church in *La Confirmation. Sens et Conjoncture Oecumenique hier et aujourd'hui* (Paris, 1973), p. 268.

6. Cf. CIC canon. 788: *ad septimum circiter aetatis annum;* cf. Pont. Rom. Ord. Conf. Praenot. No. 6.

7. E. Ruffini, in *Concilium* 4, 1968, even raises the question whether the age of confirmation should be postponed in order to prevent the danger of magical qualities being attributed to baptism in a secularized society, ibid. p. 581; cf. K. Richter, 'Firmung zwischen Taufe und Eucharistie', in *Diakonia*, art. cit., pp. 52f.; cf. for French lit. L. Ligier, op. cit., pp. 265f.

8. H. Küng, *Was ist Firmung?* (Zürich-Einsiedeln-Cologne, 1976), pp. 39 & 45.

9. Ibid., p. 39.

10. Ibid., p. 40.

11. Cf. G. Sporschill, 'Stellungnahme zur Grundtendenz der Synoden-Vorlage zur Firmpastoral', in *Arbeitsmappe Firmpastoral* (Munich & Freising, 1973), pp. 13–16, p. 15; A. Benning, *Gabe des Geistes* (Kevelaer, 1972), p. 63; G. Biemer, *Firmung*, op. cit., pp. 73–81; the General Synod of Bishops in the Federal Republic of Germany: statement, *Schwerpunkte heutiger Sakramentenpastoral*, pp. 3, 4; *Hilfen zur Firmpastoral* (1973–1976, Basle Catechetical Commission), p. 67; S. Regli, 'Firmsakrament und christliche Entfaltung', in *Mysterium Salutis*, V (Zürich-Einsiedeln-Cologne, 1976), pp. 297–348, pp. 333ff.; *Vorbereitung auf die Firmung* (Cologne, 1976), working paper 2.

12. J. Göttler, 'Das Firmalter', in *Zweiter Katechetischer Kongress* (Munich, 1928), ed. K. Schrems (Donauwörth, 1928), pp. 177–90, esp. pp. 179, 183; on twelve- to fifteen-year-olds, cf. H. Aufderbeck, 'Firmung, ein isoliertes Geschehen?' in *Zeichen des Glaubens, Festschrift für B. Fischer*, ed. H. J. Auf der Maur & B. Kleinheyer (Zürich-Freiburg, 1972), pp. 283–94; C. Herold (GDR) argues in favour of fourteen- to sixteen-year-olds in: 'Pastorale Situation und Funktion der Firmung von heute', in *Diakonia* 4 (1973), pp. 44–6.

13. Cf. O. Betz, *Sakrament der Mündigkeit* (Munich, 1968); cf. espec. L. Rohr, 'Das rechte Firmalter in psychologischer Sicht', pp. 85–100; J. Goldbrunner, P. Wes, et. al. in *Forum Firmung der Diakonia*, op. cit. (Vol I).

14. A. Exeler, 'Erwachsenenfirmung—Stunde der Wahrheit', in *Diakonia,* op. cit., p. 38–40.

15. Vatican II, *Constitution on the Sacred Liturgy,* 71; cf. the commentary by J. A. Jungmann in *Lexikon für Theologie und Kirche,* op. cit., p. 68: 'At the same time the demand was made that confirmation should be administered at an age when the personal profession of the responsibilities assumed with baptism is meaningful'; General Synod of Bishops in the Federal Republic of Germany, *Schwerpunkte Sakramentenpastoral,* op. cit., 3.4.

16. W. Kasper & K. Lehmann (*Pastorale,* I) (Mainz, 1970), p. 78.

17. Cf. G. Biemer, J. Müller & R. Zerfass, *Eingliederung in die Kirche* (Mainz, 1972), pp. 49–56; G. Biemer, *Firmung,* op. cit., pp. 28–35.

18. F. X. Arnold, *Das Gottmenschliche Prinzip der Seelsorge in Seelsorge aus der Mitte der Heilsgeschichte* (Freidburg, 1956), pp. 16–63.

19. K. Rahner, 'Sakramentale Grundlegung des Laienstandes in der Kirche' in *Schriften zur Theologie,* VII (Einsiedeln-Zürich-Cologne, 1966), pp. 330–50.

20. H. Küng, op. cit., p. 40.

21. H. A. Zwergel, *Religiöse Erziehung und Entwicklung der Persönlichkeit. Psychologischer Leitfaden für Religionslehrer und praktische Theologen* (Zürich-Einsiedeln-Cologne, 1976), p. 26.

22. 'By this is meant subsidiary learning which helps to round off or fill out incomplete structures. It arises from the desire to find a meaning for things and gives expression to the active, organizing nature of our perception' (with reference to G. W. Alport), H. A. Zwergel, op. cit., p. 46.

23. Zwergel, op. cit., p. 30.

24. P. L. Berger, *Zur Dialektik von Religion und Gesellschaft. Elemente einer soziologischen Theorie* (Frankfurt, 1973), p. 19.

25. Cf. Zwergel, op. cit., p. 38.

26. According to D. & S. Elkind, *Varieties of Religious Experience* (1962), quoted by R. J. Havighurst & W. Keating, *The Religion of Youth in Research on Religious Development. A Comprehensive Handbook,* ed. M. P. Strommen (New York, 1971), pp. 686–723; cf. Newman's conversion at this age in *Apologia Pro Vita Sua.*

27. L. Kohlberg, *Zur kognitiven Entwicklung des Kindes* (Frankfurt, 1974), pp. 60ff., cf. pp. 75f.

28. H. Nickel, *Entwicklungspsychologie des Kindes- und Jugenalters,* II, (Berne-Stuttgart-Vienna, 1975), p. 141.

29. H. A. Zwergel, op. cit., p. 45.

30. Cf. the theory of the development of the image of God by Kopps, et. al., quoted by R. J. Havighurst and B. Keating, *The Religion of Youth,* op. cit., p. 706.

31. Cf. W. Hesse's article on conscience in B. Stoeckle, *Wörterbuch christlicher Ethik* (Freiburg, 1975), pp. 114–20; p. 117.

32. Cf. G. Biemer, J. Müller and R. Zerfass, Eingliederung in die Kirche, op. cit., pp. 60–65.

Contributors

WALTER VON ARX studied theology in Lucerne, Switzerland, at the Angelicum in Rome, and at Fribourg, Switzerland. He was ordained in 1962. He is secretary of the Swiss Liturgical Commission and director of the Zürich Liturgical Institute. He has published on ritual and the sacraments.

GÜNTER BIEMER was ordained in 1955. He studied at Tübingen University and Freiburg im Breisgau, Federal Germany. He has taught in a seminary and pastoral theology at Tübingen. He is professor of educational studies and catechetics at the University of Freiburg and he has published widely on tradition and revelation, pastoral and practical theology, the teaching of world religions and catechetics.

DIONISIO BOROBIO was ordained in 1965. He studied at the Gregorian University and at the San Anselmo Liturgical Institute in Rome, and at Madrid. He is professor in the theological faculty of the University of Deusto, Spain, and director of the liturgical secretariat of the Diocese of Bilbao and a member of the Spanish Liturgical Commission. He has published on the sacraments.

AIDAN KAVANAGH, OSB, was ordained in 1957. He studied at St Meinrad Seminary, at the universities of Ottowa and Oxford and at the Faculty of Theology of the University of Trier. He was professor of liturgy at the University of Notre Dame where he founded the Murphy Centre for Liturgical Research. He is professor of liturgics in the Divinity School of Yale University.

DAVID POWER, OMI, was ordained in 1956. He is professor of liturgy at the Catholic University of America, Washington. Among his published works are *Ministers of Christ and his Church* (1969) and *Christian Priest: Elder and Prophet (1973)*.

PHILIPPE ROUILLARD, OSB, was ordained in 1962. He studied at Saint-Anselm's Athenaeum in Paris, and studied at the Lille faculty of Theology. He edited the review *La Maison-Dieu* and he now teaches sacramental theology at Saint-Anselme and at the Marianum in Rome.

JOACHIM SCHARFENBERG studied theology and philosophy and is a psychoanalyst. He was at one time in charge of a parish and a hospital chaplain. He taught at Tübingen University and became professor of practical theology at Kiel University in 1971. He has published on Freud's critique of religion, on psychoanalysis and religion, and on pastoral work.

ANTHONIUS SCHEER was ordained in 1959. He studied at the Gregorian University, Rome, and specialized in liturgical sciences at the San Anselmo Liturgical Institute. He was an associate worker for the Tilburg theological faculty for ten years and has taught at the Catholic University of Nijmegen, the Netherlands, since 1976.

KEVIN SEASOLTZ, OSB, was ordained in 1956 and professed as a Benedictine in 1960. He studied at Duquesne University, Notre Dame University, the Catholic University of America, and the Lateran University. He is professor in the School of Religious Studies at the Catholic University of America and he has published widely on liturgy and canon law.

ERICH ZENGER studied theology and oriental religions in Rome, Jerusalem, Heidelberg and Münster. Since 1972 he has been professor of Old Testament exegesis at the Ecclesiastical College in Eichstätt and since 1973 at Münster University. He has published various works on OT exegesis.